Jens Adriaan Knapp

THE ESSENCE OF PHYSICAL FITNESS TRAINING

The ultimate training manual
for advanced athletes,
developed in Germany

You are serious about
   improving and maintaining strength,
      without neglecting endurance, flexibility and joint mobility?

      Save your good health,
         save your time,
            train smart!

This book…

… is the result of over 30 years of reading, testing, discarding what is useless, and adding the best for smart physical fitness training.

In contrast to many authors, I had to combine working in different demanding fulltime-jobs *and* being a competing high level athlete at the same time.

To make it clear: I am not scientist, not an industry-sponsored sports-professional, I do not commercially help celebrities to get in shape. I do not sell any products or supplements.

I „just" know how to integrate a high level of training into the difficult situations of the *real* life.

Here just some examples of the different situations in my life:

In the 1990s I had to combine the physically hard work as a carpenter with competing in kickboxing and muay thai.

After 20 professional fights I stopped fighting being ranked #1 in germany. This was a good experience for me, but I realized, that this was not the thing I wanted to do for the rest of my life. So I made the right decision and invested more energy in my education, so that I got better and better jobs.

I met my wife, we married and quickly two nice children entered my life. The time left for training was getting short and valuable. Surprisingly i did not stop training and i did not get out of shape until today. The lack of time just forced me to reduce my training to the most important things – to the essence!

Since I was a little boy, I was looking for the ultimate manual. I wanted a manual which told me *what to do - when and how*. Here you are…

DISCLAIMER

Every instruction or activity described in this book may be
too strenuous or dangerous for some people and the readers.
The publisher and the author of this book are not responsible
 - in any manner whatsoever – for any disadvantage or
injury that may occur after following the instructions written
in this book.
Before you start, you necessarily should consult a doctor.
With the help of your doctor you can exclude individual risks.
The whole work is based on personal experience of the author.
The publisher and the author can neither guarantee the scientific
correctness of the statements, nor your success.
Individual limits or health-risks must be taken into account.
Each activity is done at your own risk!

You are not allowed to copy or reproduce parts of this book
without the permission of the publisher in any form.
Exceptions are brief quotes in reviews.

The shortcut to „Wave-style-periodization"…

Genetically you have the natural potential to build raw power and extreme endurance to catch and kill the biggest and most dangerous animals on the planet – or similar hard tasks.
Stimulate your body the right way and take the right amount of time to adapt. The result will be increasing levels of overall fitness up to your personal limit.
Increasing strength is more difficult than increasing endurance. The 2nd reason for this order is the needed time for recovery. That is why strength-training dominates the periodization.
The more energy you put into your strength-training, the less energy is left for endurance-training.
Increase the energy over four weeks and give your body one week to recover. This is a blueprint and if you need more time – do so!
To understand the concept behind the system of waving the training-energy, check the following chart.

Put this amount of energy in your training for the best results:

week:	energy for strength	energy for endurance
1	++++	-
2	-	++++
3	+	+++
4	++	++
5	+++	+
6	++++	-
7	-	++++
8	+	+++
9	++	++
10	+++	+
11	++++	-
12	to be continued...	

The shortcut to „Wave-style-endurance-training"…

week:	guidelines / what and how to do it:	energy:
1	cardio, 30-90 minutes @ 160 (-age) BPM	-
2	Performance Test	++++
3	intervals, short bursts with short active rests	+++
4	intervals, short bursts with long active rests	++
5	cardio, 30-90 minutes @ 180 (-age) BPM	+
6	cardio, 30-90 minutes @ 160 (-age) BPM	-
7	Performance Test	++++
8	intervals, short bursts with short active rests	+++
9	intervals, short bursts with long active rests	++
10	cardio, 30-90 minutes @ 180 (-age) BPM	+
11	cardio, 30-90 minutes @ 160 (-age) BPM	-
12+13	Intervals, 3-5 rounds (5 min / 60 sec)	++++

Whenever possible, wear a heartrate-monitor.
Calculate your target heart rate in BPM like this: 180-(your age).
Example: You are 35 years old > 180-35=145 BPM
BPM = (heart-) beats per minute
HR = heartrate

If you exercise without a heartrate-monitor, then do not go harder than you can handle while breathing through your nose.

In some cases it is useful, to „change the direction of the wave".
Your endurance is poor in comparison to your strength?
Endurance is much more important for you (or your goals)?
Then turn it upside down and start at week 13 and go backward!

Track your endurance-progress...

To test your *lower-body-endurance*, do the "12 Minute Run".

Your target should be 2500 m, or better more than that.

To test your upper-body-pushing-endurance, do the "push-up-test'

Your target should be 50 reps in a row, or better more than that.

To test your upper-body-pulling-endurance, do the "pull-up-test".

Your target should be 20 reps in a row, or better more than that.

Do these tests on separate days to make sure, that the results are not distorted by previous activities.

According to this, do not mix strength and endurance tests.

Testing your strenght in a state of exhaustion can lead to serious injuries. Testing is not competition. Health and safety first!

Later in this book you will find further information, how to put these tests correctly on the timeline.

Use the following chart as an overview of your results:

12-min-run / date		**push-ups / date**		**Pull-ups / date**	
2000 m	_____	30	_____	10	_____
2050 m	_____	32	_____	11	_____
2100 m	_____	34	_____	12	_____
2150 m	_____	36	_____	13	_____
2200 m	_____	38	_____	14	_____
2250 m	_____	40	_____	15	_____
2300 m	_____	42	_____	16	_____
2350 m	_____	44	_____	17	_____
2400 m	_____	46	_____	18	_____
2450 m	_____	48	_____	19	_____
2500 m	_____	50	_____	20	_____

The shortcut to „Wave-style-strength-training"…		**energy-**
week	**guidelines / what and how to do it:**	**wave:**
1	test your maximum and write it down	++++
2	time for recovery	-
3	start with calculated weights	+
4	add some weight, leverage* or reps	++
5	add some more	+++
6	test your maximum and write it down	++++
7	time for recovery	-
8	continue with new calculated weights	+
9	add some weight, leverage or reps	++
10	add some more	+++
11	test your maximum and write it down	++++
12 + 13	Take ½ of your max, very slow movements	xxxx

*Most exercises can be executed in a technical progression.
The „technical easy" type of exercise is „2", more sophisticated is „A" and very demanding exercises are „1".

<u>*Technical progression:*</u>

    2 = all the weight is on both legs and / or both arms
         example: standard push-ups

    A = most weight is on one leg and / or one arm
         example: archer push-ups on left arm and right foot

    1 = all the weight is on one leg and / or one arm
         example: one-arm-push-ups, left arm and right foot

If you want to improve from 2 over A to 1, it can be helpful to add some weight before you go to the next step of the progression (without extra weight).

You also can reduce your bodyweight with elastic bands attached to the ceiling or a pull-up bar.

Much better than guessing your weight, is to calculate it based on the experience of powerlifting-experts.

Round up/down the calculated weight to practical numbers.

As an example, you can improve a barbell-exercise like this:

week	task	Result / to-do	*calc. 1RM**	wave:
1	test, try...	3 reps @ 145 KG	*154 KG*	++++
2	recover	„light avtivity".		-
3	1RM x 0,83	5 reps @ 125 KG		+
4	1RM x 0,86	5 reps @ 130 KG		++
5	1RM x 0,88	5 reps @ 135 KG		+++
6	test, last x 0,95	5 reps @ 145 KG	*163 KG*	++++
7	recover	„light avtivity".		-
8	1RM x 0,83	5 reps @ 135 KG		+
9	1RM x 0,86	5 reps @ 140 KG		++
10	1RM x 0,88	5 reps @ 145 KG		+++
11	test, last x 0,95	4 reps @ 155 KG	*169 KG*	++++
12	1RM x 0,5	7-10 reps @ 85 KG	„plateau breaker"	
13	1RM x 0,5	7-10 reps @ 85 KG	„plateau breaker"	
14	1RM x 0,83	5 reps @ 140 KG		+
15	1RM x 0,86	to be continued...		++

Slowly, in a healthy and safe you will improve.

Follow this routine, and you will improve your strength to your genetic limits.

*The following page explains, how to calculate that.

Calculate your 1RM...

For some good reasons, you must not test your limits
with absolute maximum weight.
It must be heavy enough, so that you can not lift it
for more than 6 reps.
Take a weigt that you can lift for 2 – 6 reps.

Test-results:

1. You lifted the weight one time. A second rep ist impossible.
   The lifted weight is 100% and your 1RM.
2. You lifted the weight two times. A third rep ist impossible.
   The lifted weight is 95% of your 1RM.
   Divide the lifted weight by 0,95. This is your 1RM.
3. You lifted the weight three times. A fourth rep ist impossible.
   The lifted weight is 93% of your 1RM.
   Divide the lifted weight by 0,93. This is your 1RM
4. You lifted the weight four times. A fifth rep ist impossible.
   The lifted weight is 90% of your 1RM.
   Divide the lifted weight by 0,90. This is your 1RM
5. You lifted the weight five times. A sixth rep ist impossible.
   The lifted weight is 87% of your 1RM.
   Divide the lifted weight by 0,87. This is your 1RM
6. You lifted the weight six times. A seventh rep ist impossible.
   The lifted weight is 85% of your 1RM.
   Divide the lifted weight by 0,85. This is your 1RM

Baechle TR, Earle RW, Wathen D (2000)
Essentials of Strength Training and Conditioning, 2: 395-425

Question: A Plateau is a good thing?

Constantly improving your strength in 10-kg-steps per month would theoretically lead to 600 kg in 5 years. Also endurance… This will never happen. After some time you reach the point where you stagnate and reach a plateau.

It is a logical thing: your body reacts this way to protect itself! Your passive structures like bones and fascia need more time to adapt to more load than your muscles.

To prevent injuries, your nervous-system puts the brakes tight – you stagnate. This is a good and natural thing. Instead of using „shocking-methods", which can lead to serious injuries, you should be patient and continue with the amount of work your body can handle.

If you try to rush things, it is possible that an injury will force you to take many steps back or even stop you forever.

Be smart, be patient and accept the nature of slow progress. Only a *completely* adapted body is really strong and resilient. No one will lift a bus after one year of training. But many people can reach impressive strength at any age when training constantly smart.

Sometimes you will hear that someone „broke the plateau" with „changing and shocking". Supposedly time went on and the body adapted (delayed) during this time of „new training". You do not need scars in your muscles to bulk up your appearance. Train your slow-twitch-fibers after about 11 weeks for a duration of two weeks. This is far better than frustration. Accept time and accept your genetic limits!

Answer: YES!

Recovery...

...is as important as training!

The individually needed time can vary from 1 day to 1 week.

Guidelines to minimize recovery-time

and maximize training-frequency:

1. Do not to train to failure on „non-testing-days".
2. Do not exercise to complete exhaustion either.
3. Do not test the limit the day before explosive sport-events.
4. Avoid excessive circuit-training.
5. Avoid excessive strength-endurance-training.
6. Avoid exhausting aerobic activities taking more than 1 hou

Allowed activities:

If you like to do some „sports", or if you have to work physically, then try to stay in „light avtivity".

Your heartrate has to stay low, your muscles should not work hard and your passive structures must not be stretched. Do some joint-mobility-movements (next chapter) and / or enjoy some massage. Probably the best thing for recovery is the traditional thai-massage. An alternative is to do it with the help of a foamroller or tennis- / lacrosse-ball.

If you have any muscle-pain, then press the painful point for 3 minutes (or more) on it and move on it very slowly.

The shortcut to joint mobility...

Better than staying on the couch on „recovery-day" is to move your limbs a bit. You maintain healthy joints and activate some bloodflow in your muscles with that.

A joint-mobility-routine consists of moving each of your limbs 8 times (or more):

1. move your head in all possible directions
2. move your shoulders in forward and backward circles
3. rotate your arms in all possible directions
4. some easy push-ups with (most weight on your knees)
5. move your wrists and fingers
6. move your upper body back, forth and around
7. „hula hoop" your hips
8. some easy squats without additional weight
9. rotate your ankles in all possible directions
10. move your toes in all possible directions

A combination of two or more movements simultaneously is possible and saves some time, but it should not be exhausting. Enter the words „joint mobility", „tea-cup-movement", some ancient asian- or modern western dancing-styles into your internet-search-engine. Thai-boxers do the „wai kru".

You will be surprised about the similarities!

The the shortcut to a resilient, flexible and elastic body...

Staying completely healthy during constant strength-work and regularly aerobic exercises is not an easy task. Physical therapists have a lot of work with injuries of people who were too motivated without listening to their bodies and destroying their rotator cuff, knees and so on.

Ignoring pain, skipping necessary recovery and neglecting the passive structures is the roadmap to *nowhere*.

<u>*What you should do:*</u>

1. Practice flexibility-exercises on a separate day.
2. Warm up your body passively before and during stretching
3. Stretch your body *like a towel*.
4. Do different „forward-bending-exercises" *(roll forward)*.
5. Do different „backward-bending-exercises" *(roll back)*.
6. Do different „twisting-exercises" *(twist the towel)*.
7. Support your stretching with proper breathing.
8. Listen to your body – „pain" means „Stop! Too much!"

<u>*Examples for stretching at home:*</u>

1. Lay your back on a big exercise ball and touch the floor over your head, while your feet stay also on the floor.
2. Lay your back on a yoga-mat, walk your feet clockwise and counterclockwise in big circles around your body far over your head.
3. Do the Triangle Pose „Trikonasana".
4. Do front- and side-splits.

Proper stretching is not easy to learn. A book is not a good medium to teach that. Best choice is a „hot-yoga-class". Second best is a DVD or internet-video. You can feed the search-engine of your choice with the words „hot-yoga-class". It would be a waste of time trying to bring it correctly to paper, without a chance of transferring it in an easy and pleasant way. For that, I am honest, a teacher or a movie is far better.

The the shortcut to daily exercise…

For many people it is difficult to put the whole routine into a weekly schedule. Often the week is too short or important appointments „destroy the plan".

More important than „Monday this and Tuesday that" is to put training and recovery in the right way on the timeline. A good balance between strength, endurance and healthy passive structures (flexibility) has to be built.

You need building blocks to build up your personal routine.

Guidelines:

1. Any day can be „day 1".
2. Plan seven days for your cycle.
3. Plan more days if you need more time to recover.
4. Do not skip a routine.
5. Do not skip recovery.
6. Keep a constant order in your routine.
7. Recover 1 day (or more!) after strength-training.
8. Pushing and pulling on separate days.
9. Train pushing and pulling equally.
10. Train strength and endurance equally.
11. Practice flexibility on a separate day.
12. Do not track more than one target per day.
13. Listen to your body.

    If you feel tired: take it easy!

Remenber: Training is not „showtime"!

You want to build something.

So do not destroy something, while you train only for the goal of hard training or impressing.

The example for a good planned weekly schedule...

Wednesday	Day 1	Flexibility-training
Thursday	Day 2	Pushing-strength-training
Friday	Day 3	Recovery
Saturday	Day 4	Pulling-strength-training
Sunday	Day 5	Recovery
Monday	Day 6	Pushing-endurance-training
Tuesday	Day 7	Pulling-endurance-training
Wednesday	Day 8	Flexibility-training

...but then something comes in between. Example: You went too hard at day 4 and on day 6 you still feel totally exhausted. No problem, you continue on day 7 in the right order:

Wednesday	Day 1	Flexibility-training
Thursday	Day 2	Pushing-strength-training
Friday	Day 3	Recovery
Saturday	Day 4	Pulling-strength-training
Sunday	Day 5	Recovery
Monday	*Day 6*	*Recovery*
Tuesday	*Day 7*	*Pushing-endurance-training*
Wednesday	*Day 8*	*Pulling-endurance-training*
Thursday	*Day 9*	*Flexibility-training*

„Not enough time" to train? One day for example...

You are working in an office or similar conditions.

Ask your boss, if it is okay to do something for your health some minutes per week. Say: „I want to do something for my back."

As a routine you do your exercises spread over the day.

A strength-training day cold look like that:

6	00	get up
6	45	drive to work
7	15	start working
9	15	do one legged squats, one set each leg
9	17	have a break
9	28	do one legged squats, one set each leg
9	30	continue working
11	00	do one legged squats, one set each leg
12	30	do one legged squats, one set each leg
12	32	have a break
12	58	do one arm pushups, one set each arm
13	00	continue working
14	30	do one arm pushups, one set each arm
16	00	do one arm pushups, one set each arm
17	28	do one arm pushups, one set each arm
17	30	drive home
18	00	have a good time with your family
22	30	go to bed

You see: The time between the sets is working time! No time is wasted.

Training-time is an appointment!

Use your calendar to plan your training-time.

Many things have to be taken in account.

Your activities and your other appointments must be seen as a complete picture.

Just some rough examples, how to plan your time:

	7:00 to 17:00	evening
Mo.	work&Pushing-strength	go grocery shopping
Tu.	work	play basketball with kids
We.	work	paperwork&Pulling-strength
Th.	work	jog with your partner
Fr.	work	thai-boxing, 90min class
Sa.	Family-time	brazilian jiu jitsu, 90min class
Su.	flexibility-training	Family-time
Mo.	work&Pushing-strength	go grocery shopping
Tu.	work	45 min sport, focus on technique
We.	work&Pulling-strength	paperwork or get things done
Th.	work	45 min sport, focus on technique
Fr.	work	thai-boxing, 90min class
Sa.	Family-time	brazilian jiu jitsu, 90min class
Su.	flexibility-training	Family-time
Mo.	work	thai-boxing, 90min class
Tu.	work	brazilian jiu jitsu, 90min class
We.	work&flexibility-training	go grocery shopping
Th.	work&Pushing-strength	get things done
Fr.	work	ride your bike&meet friends
Sa.	pulling-strength with friends	Party-time: Dance!
Su.	ride your bike back home...	

Track your strength-progress...

...and keep your strength in balance!

The following chart must be seen as a „ladder". Going down one row is „easy-tracking your improvement". For balanced strenght, you complete each row at first with a one rep max (or your calculated 1RM). Move to the next row when 5 are easily done.

recommended targets for the main lifts:

squat, target = 2 x BW

deadlift, target = 2,8 x BW

push-up (weight on both hands, total), target = 1,5 x BW

pull-up (weight on both hands, total), target = 1,5 x BW

Climb the ladder of weight in KG!

squat	deadlift	push-up	pull-up	date
80	110	60	60	_____
82,5	115	62,5	62,5	_____
87,5	120	65	65	_____
90	125	67,5	67,5	_____
92,5	130	70	70	_____
95	135	72,5	72,5	_____
100	140	75	75	_____
105	145	77,5	77,5	_____
105	150	80	80	_____
110	155	82,5	82,5	_____
115	160	85	85	_____
115	165	87,5	87,5	_____
120	170	90	90	_____
125	175	92,5	92,5	_____
125	180	95	95	_____

squat	deadlift	push-up	pull-up	date
130	185	97,5	97,5	_____
135	190	100	100	_____
140	195	105	105	_____
145	205	110	110	_____
155	215	115	115	_____
160	225	120	120	_____
165	235	125	125	_____
175	245	130	130	_____
180	250	135	135	_____
185	260	140	140	_____
195	270	145	145	_____
200	280	150	150	_____
205	290	155	155	_____
215	300	160	160	_____
220	310	165	165	_____
225	320	170	170	_____
235	330	175	175	_____
240	340	180	180	_____

The shortcut to bodyweight improvement...

You *want* or *have to* loose weight?

A guideline for healthy weight-loss is to give your body each day 500 Kalories less than required. This is a question of proper nutrition and macro-nutritients-management.

That could fill another book.

Done properly this leads to a weight-loss of 0,5 KG per week.

The essence is to track your bodyweight and to reach your weekly target-weight. Example: The following schedule shows an athlete, who wants to loose 5 Kgs without compromising fitness.

WEEK	BW-GOAL	SCALED BW	DATE	
1	90,0 KG	90,0 KG	30.	Jan.
2	89,5 KG	88,7 KG	7.	Jan.
3	89,0 KG	89,2 KG	14.	Jan.
4	88,5 KG	88,8 KG	21.	Jan.
5	88,0 KG	88,2 KG	28.	Jan.
6	87,5 KG	88,0 KG	4.	Feb.
7	87,0 KG	87,3 KG	11.	Feb.
8	86,5 KG	87,0 KG	18.	Feb.
9	86,0 KG	86,5 KG	25.	Feb.
10	85,5 KG	85,9 KG	2.	Mar.
11	85,0 KG	85,5 KG	9.	Mar.
12		85,1 KG	16.	Mar.
13		85,0 KG	23.	Mar.

Okay, two weeks later than planned...

But the athlete did it the right way, because his goal was to lose the weight slowly without compromising his health.

The following two pages are for your 1-year-BW-tracking.

Your BW:

WEEK	BW-GOAL	SCALED BW	DATE
1	_____ KG	_____ KG	_____
2	_____ KG	_____ KG	_____
3	_____ KG	_____ KG	_____
4	_____ KG	_____ KG	_____
5	_____ KG	_____ KG	_____
6	_____ KG	_____ KG	_____
7	_____ KG	_____ KG	_____
8	_____ KG	_____ KG	_____
9	_____ KG	_____ KG	_____
10	_____ KG	_____ KG	_____
11	_____ KG	_____ KG	_____
12	_____ KG	_____ KG	_____
13	_____ KG	_____ KG	_____
14	_____ KG	_____ KG	_____
15	_____ KG	_____ KG	_____
16	_____ KG	_____ KG	_____
17	_____ KG	_____ KG	_____
18	_____ KG	_____ KG	_____
19	_____ KG	_____ KG	_____
20	_____ KG	_____ KG	_____
21	_____ KG	_____ KG	_____
22	_____ KG	_____ KG	_____
23	_____ KG	_____ KG	_____
24	_____ KG	_____ KG	_____
25	_____ KG	_____ KG	_____
26	_____ KG	_____ KG	_____

Your BW:

WEEK	BW-GOAL	SCALED BW	DATE
27	_____ KG	_____ KG	_____
28	_____ KG	_____ KG	_____
29	_____ KG	_____ KG	_____
30	_____ KG	_____ KG	_____
31	_____ KG	_____ KG	_____
32	_____ KG	_____ KG	_____
33	_____ KG	_____ KG	_____
34	_____ KG	_____ KG	_____
35	_____ KG	_____ KG	_____
36	_____ KG	_____ KG	_____
37	_____ KG	_____ KG	_____
38	_____ KG	_____ KG	_____
39	_____ KG	_____ KG	_____
40	_____ KG	_____ KG	_____
41	_____ KG	_____ KG	_____
42	_____ KG	_____ KG	_____
43	_____ KG	_____ KG	_____
44	_____ KG	_____ KG	_____
45	_____ KG	_____ KG	_____
46	_____ KG	_____ KG	_____
47	_____ KG	_____ KG	_____
48	_____ KG	_____ KG	_____
49	_____ KG	_____ KG	_____
50	_____ KG	_____ KG	_____
51	_____ KG	_____ KG	_____
52	_____ KG	_____ KG	_____

Instead of endless theory, we put it all together…

…a complete blueprint for your training-schedule!

Do the recommended exercises

until you are through the whole program.

Check your rest-heart-rate (R-RH)

every morning to avoid overtraining.

This ist not a book to read sitting on the couch...

...read the instructions for one day and do it!

Flexibility-training   `Day 1`   **R-HR___**   **energy: +**

The best choice is a „hot-yoga-class". No yoga-class available?
A good yoga-video-instructional can help to „do it right".
No yoga-class or video available? No problem! Do this:

Remember:

#1 Listen to your body – „pain" means „Stop! Too much!"

#2 Warm up your body passively before stretching.

#3 Wear warm clothes or heat your room for staying warm.

#4 Support your stretching with proper breathing:

Hold position > breathe in > simultaneously breath out and go deeper into the position > hold position > simultaneousl breath out and go deeper into the position > repeat slowly

target:	the backside of your body
to do:	Do different „forward-bending-exercises".
example:	Lay your back on the floor. Walk your feet slowly clockwise in a big circle around your body far over your head. Repeat the same thing counterclockwise.
target:	the frontside of your body
to do:	Do different „backward-bending-exercises".
example:	Lay your back on a exercise ball and touch the floor over your head, while your feet stay also on the floor. Walk your hands as close as possible in direction to your feet. Bridge as high as possible and hold >20 sec.
target:	your trunk, your hips and your glutes
to do:	Do different „twisting- and splitting exercises".
example:	Do the Triangle Pose „Trikonasana". Do the Half Spinal Twist Pose „Ardha Matsyendrasana' Do front- and side-splits.

Pushing-strength `Day 2` R-HR____ test ++++

Be careful with testing!

Only test your strength fully recovered!

guidelines / what and how to do it:

Exercise-speed: fast (controlled)   Breaks: 3 to 10 minutes

Set	weight	reps
1	multiply your expected 1RM by 0,6	5
2	multiply your expected 1RM by 0,7	5
3	multiply your expected 1RM by 0,8	3
4	multiply your expected 1RM by 0,9	amrap*

amrap = as many reps as possible

Set	exercise	progr.	Result, reps / weight	calc. 1RM*
1	squat	2/A/1	____ @ ____ KG	
2	squat	2/A/1	____ @ ____ KG	
3	squat	2/A/1	____ @ ____ KG	
4	**squat**	2/A/1	____ @ ____ KG	____**KG**
1	dip	2/A/1	____ @ ____ KG	
2	dip	2/A/1	____ @ ____ KG	
3	dip	2/A/1	____ @ ____ KG	
4	**dip**	2/A/1	____ @ ____ KG	____**KG**
1	overhead press	2/A/1	____ @ ____ KG	
2	overhead press	2/A/1	____ @ ____ KG	
3	overhead press	2/A/1	____ @ ____ KG	
4	**overhead press**	2/A/1	____ @ ____ KG	____**KG**
1	push-up	2/A/1	____ @ ____ KG	
2	push-up	2/A/1	____ @ ____ KG	
3	push-up	2/A/1	____ @ ____ KG	
4	**push-up**	2/A/1	____ @ ____ KG	____**KG**

Recovery **Day 3** R-HR____   energy: -

<u>guidelines / what and how to do it:</u>

Probably the best thing to do now is the traditional thai-massage.

If a massage is not availabe, do the joint-mobility-routine.

If you have any muscle-pain, then press the painful point with a foamroller or tennis- / lacrosse-ball for 3 minutes (or more) on it and move on it very slowly.

If you like to do some „sports", or if you have to work physically, then try to stay in „light avtivity".

<u>Remember:</u>

#1 Your heartrate has to stay low, your muscles should not work hard and your passive structures must not be stretched.

#2 keep heart rate lower than BPM: 160-(your age)=_____

#3 If you exercise without a HR-monitor, then do not go harder than you can handle while breathing through your nose. It must feel light / easy to maintain the activity.

#4 Take a look at your rest-heart-rate:

>5 BPM more than normal? Take it easy!

>10 BPM more than normal? You need more than one day for recovery!

Pulling-strength **Day 4** R-HR____ test ++++

guidelines / what and how to do it:

Exercise-speed: fast (controlled)   Breaks: 3 to 10 minutes

Set	weight	reps
1	multiply your expected 1RM by 0,6	5
2	multiply your expected 1RM by 0,7	5
3	multiply your expected 1RM by 0,8	3
4	multiply your expected 1RM by 0,9	amrap*

amrap = as many reps as possible

Set	exercise	progr.	Result, reps / weight	calc. 1RM*
1	deadlift	2/A/1	____ @ ____ KG	
2	deadlift	2/A/1	____ @ ____ KG	
3	deadlift	2/A/1	____ @ ____ KG	
4	**deadlift**	2/A/1	____ @ ____ KG	_____**KG**
1	pull-up	2/A/1	____ @ ____ KG	
2	pull-up	2/A/1	____ @ ____ KG	
3	pull-up	2/A/1	____ @ ____ KG	
4	**pull-up**	2/A/1	____ @ ____ KG	_____**KG**
1	hang clean	2/A/1	____ @ ____ KG	
2	hang clean	2/A/1	____ @ ____ KG	
3	hang clean	2/A/1	____ @ ____ KG	
4	**hang clean**	2/A/1	____ @ ____ KG	_____**KG**
1	body row	2/A/1	____ @ ____ KG	
2	body row	2/A/1	____ @ ____ KG	
3	body row	2/A/1	____ @ ____ KG	
4	**body row**	2/A/1	____ @ ____ KG	_____**KG**

Recovery   **Day 5**   R-HR____energy: -

guidelines / what and how to do it:

Probably the best thing to do now is the traditional thai-massage.

If a massage is not availabe, do the joint-mobility-routine.

If you have any muscle-pain, then press the painful point with a foamroller or tennis- / lacrosse-ball for 3 minutes (or more) on it and move on it very slowly.

If you like to do some „sports", or if you have to work physically, then try to stay in „light avtivity".

Remember:

#1 Your heartrate has to stay low, your muscles should not work hard and your passive structures must not be stretched.

#2   keep heart rate lower than BPM: 160-(your age)=_____

#3 If you exercise without a HR-monitor, then do not go harder than you can handle while breathing through your nose. It must feel light / easy to maintain the activity.

#4 Take a look at your rest-heart-rate:

>5 BPM more than normal? Take it easy!

>10 BPM more than normal? You need more than one day for recovery!

Pushing-endurance `Day 6` **R-HR___energy:** -

30 to 90 minutes light activities.

Possible activities are jogging, cycling, dancing, shadow-boxing, Rope-skipping and any sports using the arobic energy-system.

<u>*Remember:*</u>
- #1 When ever possible, wear a heartrate-monitor.
- #2 keep heart rate in BPM: 160-(your age)=_____
- #3 If you exercise without a HR-monitor, then do not go harder than you can handle while breathing through your nose. It must feel light / easy to maintain the activity.

Pulling-endurance `Day 7` **R-HR___energy:** -

30 to 90 minutes light activities.

Possible activities are swimming, rowing, climbing, ski-long-run and any sports using the arobic energy-system.

Remember:
- #1 When ever possible, wear a heartrate-monitor.
- #2 keep heart rate in BPM: 160-(your age)=_____
- #3 If you exercise without a HR-monitor, then do not go harder than you can handle while breathing through your nose. It must feel light / easy to maintain the activity.

Flexibility-training   `Day 8`   **R-HR___energy:**   **+**

The best choice is a „hot-yoga-class". No yoga-class available?

A good yoga-video-instructional can help to „do it right".

No yoga-class or video available? No problem! Do this:

> *Remember:*
>
> *#1 Listen to your body – „pain" means „Stop! Too much!"*
>
> *#2 Warm up your body passively before stretching.*
>
> *#3 Wear warm clothes or heat your room for staying warm.*
>
> *#4 Support your stretching with proper breathing:*
>
> *Hold position > breathe in > simultaneously breath out and go deeper into the position > hold position > simultaneousl breath out and go deeper into the position > repeat slowly*

target: the backside of your body

to do: Do different „forward-bending-exercises".

example: Lay your back on the floor. Walk your feet slowly clockwise in a big circle around your body far over your head. Repeat the same thing counterclockwise.

target: the frontside of your body

to do: Do different „backward-bending-exercises".

example: Lay your back on a exercise ball and touch the floor over your head, while your feet stay also on the floor. Walk your hands as close as possible in direction to your feet. Bridge as high as possible and hold >20 sec.

target: your trunk, your hips and your glutes

to do: Do different „twisting- and splitting exercises".

example: Do the Triangle Pose „Trikonasana".
Do the Half Spinal Twist Pose „Ardha Matsyendrasana'
Do front- and side-splits.

Pushing-strength **Day 9** **R-HR___energy:**   -

guidelines / what and how to do it:

Exercise-speed: moderate   Breaks: 3 to 10 minutes

Set	weight	reps
1	multiply your 1RM by 0,5	5
2	multiply your 1RM by 0,6	5
3	multiply your 1RM by 0,7	5

Set	exercise	progr.	Result, reps / weight	calc. 1RM*
1	squat	2/A/1	____ @ ____ KG	
2	squat	2/A/1	____ @ ____ KG	
3	squat	2/A/1	____ @ ____ KG	
1	dip	2/A/1	____ @ ____ KG	
2	dip	2/A/1	____ @ ____ KG	
3	dip	2/A/1	____ @ ____ KG	
1	overhead press	2/A/1	____ @ ____ KG	
2	overhead press	2/A/1	____ @ ____ KG	
3	overhead press	2/A/1	____ @ ____ KG	
1	push-up	2/A/1	____ @ ____ KG	
2	push-up	2/A/1	____ @ ____ KG	
3	push-up	2/A/1	____ @ ____ KG	

Recovery   **Day 10**   R-HR____energy: -

guidelines / what and how to do it:

Probably the best thing to do now is the traditional thai-massage.

If a massage is not availabe, do the joint-mobility-routine.

If you have any muscle-pain, then press the painful point with a foamroller or tennis- / lacrosse-ball for 3 minutes (or more) on it and move on it very slowly.

If you like to do some „sports", or if you have to work physically, then try to stay in „light avtivity".

Remember:

#1 Your heartrate has to stay low, your muscles should not work hard and your passive structures must not be stretched.

#2   keep heart rate lower than BPM: 160-(your age)=_____

#3 If you exercise without a HR-monitor, then do not go harder than you can handle while breathing through your nose. It must feel light / easy to maintain the activity.

#4 Take a look at your rest-heart-rate:

      >5 BPM more than normal? Take it easy!

      >10 BPM more than normal? You need more than one day for recovery!

Pulling-strength   **Day 11**   R-HR___energy: -

guidelines / what and how to do it:

Exercise-speed: moderate   Breaks: 3 to 10 minutes

Set	weight	reps
1	multiply your 1RM by 0,5	5
2	multiply your 1RM by 0,6	5
3	multiply your 1RM by 0,7	5

Set	exercise	progr.	Result, reps / weight	calc. 1RM*
1	deadlift	2/A/1	____ @ ____ KG	
2	deadlift	2/A/1	____ @ ____ KG	
3	deadlift	2/A/1	____ @ ____ KG	
1	pull-up	2/A/1	____ @ ____ KG	
2	pull-up	2/A/1	____ @ ____ KG	
3	pull-up	2/A/1	____ @ ____ KG	
1	hang clean	2/A/1	____ @ ____ KG	
2	hang clean	2/A/1	____ @ ____ KG	
3	hang clean	2/A/1	____ @ ____ KG	
1	body row	2/A/1	____ @ ____ KG	
2	body row	2/A/1	____ @ ____ KG	
3	body row	2/A/1	____ @ ____ KG	

Recovery **Day 12**   R-HR___energy: -

<u>guidelines / what and how to do it:</u>

Probably the best thing to do now is the traditional thai-massage.

If a massage is not availabe, do the joint-mobility-routine.

If you have any muscle-pain, then press the painful point with a foamroller or tennis- / lacrosse-ball for 3 minutes (or more) on it and move on it very slowly.

If you like to do some „sports", or if you have to work physically, then try to stay in „light avtivity".

<u>*Remember:*</u>

#1 Your heartrate has to stay low, your muscles should not work hard and your passive structures must not be stretched.

#2   keep heart rate lower than BPM: 160-(your age)=_____

#3 If you exercise without a HR-monitor, then do not go harder than you can handle while breathing through your nose. It must feel light / easy to maintain the activity.

#4 Take a look at your rest-heart-rate:

>5 BPM more than normal? Take it easy!

>10 BPM more than normal? You need more than one day for recovery!

Pushing-endurance   `Day 13`   R-HR____   Test ++++

To test your *lower-body-endurance*, do the "12 Minute Run".
Your target should be 2500 m, or better more than that.

Rest for as long as possible (if possible more than 10 minutes).

To test your upper-body-pushing-endurance, do the "push-up-test'
Your target should be 50 reps in a row, or better more than that.

Track your progress!

Remember:
#1 When ever possible, wear a heartrate-monitor.
#2 target heart rate in BPM: 180-(your age)=_____
#3 If you exercise without a HR-monitor, then do not go harder than you can handle while breathing through your *nose.*
#4 Testing your strenght in a state of exhaustion can lead to serious injuries.
#5 Be careful with previous activities.
#6 Do not mix strength and endurance tests.
#7 Testing is not competition. Health and safety first!

    your score: 12-min-run   ____   m

                               push-ups   ____   reps

Pulling-endurance `Day 14` R-HR____ Test ++++

To test your upper-body-pulling-endurance, do the "pull-up-test". Your target should be 20 reps in a row, or better more than that.

Track your progress!

Remember:

#1 Testing your strenght in a state of exhaustion can lead to serious injuries.
#2 Be careful with previous activities.
#3 Do not mix strength and endurance tests.
#4 Testing is not competition. Health and safety first!

your score: pull-ups   ____   reps

Flexibility-training   `Day 15`   **R-HR___energy: +**

The best choice is a „hot-yoga-class". No yoga-class available?

A good yoga-video-instructional can help to „do it right".

No yoga-class or video available? No problem! Do this:

> *Remember:*
>
> *#1 Listen to your body – „pain" means „Stop! Too much!"*
>
> *#2 Warm up your body passively before stretching.*
>
> *#3 Wear warm clothes or heat your room for staying warm.*
>
> *#4 Support your stretching with proper breathing:*
>
> *Hold position > breathe in > simultaneously breath out and go deeper into the position > hold position > simultaneousl*y *breath out and go deeper into the position > repeat slowly*

target:	the backside of your body

to do: Do different „forward-bending-exercises".

example: Lay your back on the floor. Walk your feet slowly clockwise in a big circle around your body far over your head. Repeat the same thing counterclockwise.

target:	the frontside of your body

to do: Do different „backward-bending-exercises".

example: Lay your back on a exercise ball and touch the floor over your head, while your feet stay also on the floor. Walk your hands as close as possible in direction to your feet. Bridge as high as possible and hold >20 sec.

target:	your trunk, your hips and your glutes

to do: Do different „twisting- and splitting exercises".

example: Do the Triangle Pose „Trikonasana".

Do the Half Spinal Twist Pose „Ardha Matsyendrasana'

Do front- and side-splits.

Pushing-strength **Day 16** R-HR___energy: +

guidelines / what and how to do it:

Exercise-speed: fast (controlled)   Breaks: 3 to 10 minutes

Set	weight	reps
1	multiply your 1RM by 0,5	5
2	multiply your 1RM by 0,6	5
3	multiply your 1RM by 0,7	5
4	multiply your 1RM by 0,83	5

Set	exercise	progr.	Result, reps / weight
1	squat	2/A/1	____ @ ____ KG
2	squat	2/A/1	____ @ ____ KG
3	squat	2/A/1	____ @ ____ KG
4	**squat**	2/A/1	____ @ ____ KG
1	dip	2/A/1	____ @ ____ KG
2	dip	2/A/1	____ @ ____ KG
3	dip	2/A/1	____ @ ____ KG
4	**dip**	2/A/1	____ @ ____ KG
1	overhead press	2/A/1	____ @ ____ KG
2	overhead press	2/A/1	____ @ ____ KG
3	overhead press	2/A/1	____ @ ____ KG
4	**overhead press**	2/A/1	____ @ ____ KG
1	push-up	2/A/1	____ @ ____ KG
2	push-up	2/A/1	____ @ ____ KG
3	push-up	2/A/1	____ @ ____ KG
4	**push-up**	2/A/1	____ @ ____ KG

Recovery   **Day 17**   **R-HR___energy:**   -

<u>*guidelines / what and how to do it:*</u>

Probably the best thing to do now is the traditional thai-massage.

If a massage is not availabe, do the joint-mobility-routine.

If you have any muscle-pain, then press the painful point with a foamroller or tennis- / lacrosse-ball for 3 minutes (or more) on it and move on it very slowly.

If you like to do some „sports", or if you have to work physically, then try to stay in „light avtivity".

<u>*Remember:*</u>

#1   Your heartrate has to stay low, your muscles should not work hard and your passive structures must not be stretched.

#2   keep heart rate lower than BPM: 160-(your age)=_____

#3   If you exercise without a HR-monitor, then do not go harder than you can handle while breathing through your nose. It must feel light / easy to maintain the activity.

#4   Take a look at your rest-heart-rate:

        >5 BPM more than normal? Take it easy!

        >10 BPM more than normal? You need more than one day for recovery!

Pulling-strength **Day 18** R-HR___energy: +

guidelines / what and how to do it:

Exercise-speed: fast (controlled) Breaks: 3 to 10 minutes

Set	weight	reps
1	multiply your 1RM by 0,5	5
2	multiply your 1RM by 0,6	5
3	multiply your 1RM by 0,7	5
4	multiply your 1RM by 0,83	5

Set	exercise	progr.	Result, reps / weight	calc. 1RM*
1	deadlift	2/A/1	____ @ ____ KG	
2	deadlift	2/A/1	____ @ ____ KG	
3	deadlift	2/A/1	____ @ ____ KG	
4	**deadlift**	2/A/1	____ @ ____ KG	
1	pull-up	2/A/1	____ @ ____ KG	
2	pull-up	2/A/1	____ @ ____ KG	
3	pull-up	2/A/1	____ @ ____ KG	
4	**pull-up**	2/A/1	____ @ ____ KG	
1	hang clean	2/A/1	____ @ ____ KG	
2	hang clean	2/A/1	____ @ ____ KG	
3	hang clean	2/A/1	____ @ ____ KG	
4	**hang clean**	2/A/1	____ @ ____ KG	
1	body row	2/A/1	____ @ ____ KG	
2	body row	2/A/1	____ @ ____ KG	
3	body row	2/A/1	____ @ ____ KG	
4	**body row**	2/A/1	____ @ ____ KG	

Recovery **Day 19**   R-HR___energy: -

guidelines / what and how to do it:

Probably the best thing to do now is the traditional thai-massage.

If a massage is not availabe, do the joint-mobility-routine.

If you have any muscle-pain, then press the painful point with a foamroller or tennis- / lacrosse-ball for 3 minutes (or more) on it and move on it very slowly.

If you like to do some „sports", or if you have to work physically, then try to stay in „light avtivity".

Remember:

#1 Your heartrate has to stay low, your muscles should not work hard and your passive structures must not be stretched.

#2 keep heart rate lower than BPM: 160-(your age)=_____

#3 If you exercise without a HR-monitor, then do not go harder than you can handle while breathing through your nose. It must feel light / easy to maintain the activity.

#4 Take a look at your rest-heart-rate:

>5 BPM more than normal? Take it easy!

>10 BPM more than normal? You need more than one day for recovery!

Pushing-endurance `Day 20` **R-HR___energy: +++**
intervals, short bursts with short active rests

guidelines / what and how to do it:

If you have access to a heavy punching-bag (or better a training-partner with pads), the best option ist to do punching and kicking. No bag and no partner? Very good activities are burpees, rope-skipping, sprinting and cycling.

Since these activities (except of burpees) do not target the upper body, do explosive push-ups after a 3-10 min rest.

To do these intervals effectively, alternate between short burst of explosive power-movements and slow / easy paced activity.

Set your interval-timer: rounds= 10-20
Round-length= 15 sec
active rest= 15 sec

During the round: go hard and fast!
During the active rest: move in a loose way and breathe!

Remember:

#1 *When ever possible, wear a heartrate-monitor.*

#2 *target heart rate in BPM: 180-(your age)=_____*

#3 *If you exercise without a HR-monitor, then do not go harder than you can handle while breathing through your nose.*

#4 *take longer rests if #2 or #3 is not possible.*

Pulling-endurance   **Day 21**   **R-HR___ energy: +++**
intervals, short bursts with short active rests

guidelines / what and how to do it:

Very good activities for this kind of training are swimming, rowing, climbing (ropes), pull-ups, heavy ropes, ski run long and Kettlebell-snatches.

To do these intervals effectively, alternate between short burst of explosive power-movements and slow / easy paced activity.

Set your interval-timer: **rounds= 10-20**
                   Round-length= 15 sec
                       active rest= 15 sec

During the round: go hard and fast!
During the active rest: move in a loose way and breathe!

Remember:

#1 When ever possible, wear a heartrate-monitor.

#2 target heart rate in BPM: 180-(your age)=_____

#3 If you exercise without a HR-monitor, then do not go harder than you can handle while breathing through your nose.

#4 take longer rests if #2 or #3 is not possible.

Flexibility-training   `Day 22`   **R-HR___energy:**   **+**

The best choice is a „hot-yoga-class". No yoga-class available?

A good yoga-video-instructional can help to „do it right".

No yoga-class or video available? No problem! Do this:

Remember:

#1 Listen to your body – „pain" means „Stop! Too much!"

#2 Warm up your body passively before stretching.

#3 Wear warm clothes or heat your room for staying warm.

#4 Support your stretching with proper breathing:

Hold position > breathe in > simultaneously breath out and go deeper into the position > hold position > simultaneousl breath out and go deeper into the position > repeat slowly

target:	the backside of your body

to do: Do different „forward-bending-exercises".

example: Lay your back on the floor. Walk your feet slowly clockwise in a big circle around your body far over your head. Repeat the same thing counterclockwise.

target:	the frontside of your body

to do: Do different „backward-bending-exercises".

example: Lay your back on a exercise ball and touch the floor over your head, while your feet stay also on the floor. Walk your hands as close as possible in direction to your feet. Bridge as high as possible and hold >20 sec.

target:	your trunk, your hips and your glutes

to do: Do different „twisting- and splitting exercises".

example: Do the Triangle Pose „Trikonasana".

Do the Half Spinal Twist Pose „Ardha Matsyendrasana'

Do front- and side-splits.

| Pushing-strength | **Day 23** | R-HR___ energy: ++ |

guidelines / what and how to do it:

Exercise-speed: fast (controlled)   Breaks: 3 to 10 minutes

Set	weight	reps
1	multiply your 1RM by 0,5	5
2	multiply your 1RM by 0,6	5
3	multiply your 1RM by 0,7	5
4	multiply your 1RM by 0,86	3-4

Set	exercise	progr.	Result, reps / weight
1	squat	2/A/1	____ @ ____ KG
2	squat	2/A/1	____ @ ____ KG
3	squat	2/A/1	____ @ ____ KG
4	**squat**	2/A/1	____ @ ____ KG
1	dip	2/A/1	____ @ ____ KG
2	dip	2/A/1	____ @ ____ KG
3	dip	2/A/1	____ @ ____ KG
4	**dip**	2/A/1	____ @ ____ KG
1	overhead press	2/A/1	____ @ ____ KG
2	overhead press	2/A/1	____ @ ____ KG
3	overhead press	2/A/1	____ @ ____ KG
4	**overhead press**	2/A/1	____ @ ____ KG
1	push-up	2/A/1	____ @ ____ KG
2	push-up	2/A/1	____ @ ____ KG
3	push-up	2/A/1	____ @ ____ KG
4	**push-up**	2/A/1	____ @ ____ KG

#1 *Do not to train to failure on „non-testing-days".*

#2 *Do not exercise to complete exhaustion either.*

Recovery — Day 24 R-HR___ energy: -

guidelines / what and how to do it:

Probably the best thing to do now is the traditional thai-massage.

If a massage is not availabe, do the joint-mobility-routine.

If you have any muscle-pain, then press the painful point with a foamroller or tennis- / lacrosse-ball for 3 minutes (or more) on it and move on it very slowly.

If you like to do some „sports", or if you have to work physically, then try to stay in „light avtivity".

Remember:

#1 Your heartrate has to stay low, your muscles should not work hard and your passive structures must not be stretched.

#2 keep heart rate lower than BPM: 160-(your age)=_____

#3 If you exercise without a HR-monitor, then do not go harder than you can handle while breathing through your nose. It must feel light / easy to maintain the activity.

#4 Take a look at your rest-heart-rate:
>5 BPM more than normal? Take it easy!
>10 BPM more than normal? You need more than one day for recovery!

Pulling-strength **Day 25** **R-HR___ energy:** ++

guidelines / what and how to do it:

Exercise-speed: fast (controlled)   Breaks: 3 to 10 minutes

Set	weight	reps
1	multiply your 1RM by 0,5	5
2	multiply your 1RM by 0,6	5
3	multiply your 1RM by 0,7	5
4	multiply your 1RM by 0,86	3-4

Set	exercise	progr.	Result, reps / weight	calc. 1RM*
1	deadlift	2/A/1	____ @ ____ KG	
2	deadlift	2/A/1	____ @ ____ KG	
3	deadlift	2/A/1	____ @ ____ KG	
4	**deadlift**	2/A/1	____ @ ____ KG	
1	pull-up	2/A/1	____ @ ____ KG	
2	pull-up	2/A/1	____ @ ____ KG	
3	pull-up	2/A/1	____ @ ____ KG	
4	**pull-up**	2/A/1	____ @ ____ KG	
1	hang clean	2/A/1	____ @ ____ KG	
2	hang clean	2/A/1	____ @ ____ KG	
3	hang clean	2/A/1	____ @ ____ KG	
4	**hang clean**	2/A/1	____ @ ____ KG	
1	body row	2/A/1	____ @ ____ KG	
2	body row	2/A/1	____ @ ____ KG	
3	body row	2/A/1	____ @ ____ KG	
4	**body row**	2/A/1	____ @ ____ KG	

#1 *Do not to train to failure on „non-testing-days".*

#2 *Do not exercise to complete exhaustion either.*

Recovery   **Day 26**   **R-HR___energy:** -

guidelines / what and how to do it:

Probably the best thing to do now is the traditional thai-massage.

If a massage is not availabe, do the joint-mobility-routine.

If you have any muscle-pain, then press the painful point with a foamroller or tennis- / lacrosse-ball for 3 minutes (or more) on it and move on it very slowly.

If you like to do some „sports", or if you have to work physically, then try to stay in „light avtivity".

Remember:

#1 Your heartrate has to stay low, your muscles should not work hard and your passive structures must not be stretched.

#2 keep heart rate lower than BPM: 160-(your age)=_____

#3 If you exercise without a HR-monitor, then do not go harder than you can handle while breathing through your nose. It must feel light / easy to maintain the activity.

#4 Take a look at your rest-heart-rate:

>5 BPM more than normal? Take it easy!

>10 BPM more than normal? You need more than one day for recovery!

Pushing-endurance `Day 27` **R-HR___energy: ++**
intervals, short bursts with long active rests

guidelines / what and how to do it:

If you have access to a heavy punching-bag (or better a training-partner with pads), the best option ist to do punching and kicking. No bag and no partner? Very good activities are burpees, rope-skipping, sprinting and cycling.

Since these activities (except of burpees) do not target the upper body, do explosive push-ups after a 3-10 min rest. To do these intervals effectively, alternate between short burst of explosive power-movements and slow / easy paced activity.

Set your interval-timer: rounds= 10-20
Round-length= 10 sec
active rest= 40-90 sec

During the round: go hard and fast!
During the active rest: move in a loose way and breathe!

Remember:

#1 When ever possible, wear a heartrate-monitor.

#2 target heart rate in BPM: 180-(your age)=_____

#3 If you exercise without a HR-monitor, then do not go harder than you can handle while breathing through your nose.

#4 take longer rests if #2 or #3 is not possible.

Pulling-endurance   **Day 28**   **R-HR___energy:**   **++**

intervals, short bursts with long active rests

guidelines / what and how to do it:

Very good activities for this kind of training are swimming, rowing, climbing (ropes), pull-ups, heavy ropes, ski run long and Kettlebell-snatches.

To do these intervals effectively, alternate between short burst of explosive power-movements and slow / easy paced activity.

Set your interval-timer: **rounds= 10-20**

Round-length= 10 sec

active rest= 40-90 sec

During the round: go hard and fast!

During the active rest: move in a loose way and breathe!

Remember:

#1 *When ever possible, wear a heartrate-monitor.*

#2 *target heart rate in BPM: 180-(your age)=_____*

#3 *If you exercise without a HR-monitor, then do not go harder than you can handle while breathing through your nose.*

#4 take longer rests if #2 or #3 is not possible.

Flexibility-training   `Day 29`   **R-HR___energy: +**

The best choice is a „hot-yoga-class". No yoga-class available?
A good yoga-video-instructional can help to „do it right".
No yoga-class or video available? No problem! Do this:

Remember:

#1 Listen to your body – „pain" means „Stop! Too much!"

#2 Warm up your body passively before stretching.

#3 Wear warm clothes or heat your room for staying warm.

#4 Support your stretching with proper breathing:

Hold position > breathe in > simultaneously breath out and go deeper into the position > hold position > simultaneousl, *breath out and go deeper into the position > repeat slowly*

target:	the backside of your body

to do: Do different „forward-bending-exercises".

example: Lay your back on the floor. Walk your feet slowly clockwise in a big circle around your body far over your head. Repeat the same thing counterclockwise.

target:	the frontside of your body

to do: Do different „backward-bending-exercises".

example: Lay your back on a exercise ball and touch the floor over your head, while your feet stay also on the floor. Walk your hands as close as possible in direction to your feet. Bridge as high as possible and hold >20 sec.

target:	your trunk, your hips and your glutes

to do: Do different „twisting- and splitting exercises".

example: Do the Triangle Pose „Trikonasana".
Do the Half Spinal Twist Pose „Ardha Matsyendrasana'
Do front- and side-splits.

Pushing-strength **Day 30**   R-HR___ energy: **+++**

guidelines / what and how to do it:

Exercise-speed: fast (controlled)   Breaks: 3 to 10 minutes

Set	weight	reps
1	multiply your 1RM by 0,5	5
2	multiply your 1RM by 0,6	5
3	multiply your 1RM by 0,7	5
4	multiply your 1RM by 0,88	3-4

Set	exercise	progr.	Result, reps / weight
1	squat	2/A/1	____ @ ____ KG
2	squat	2/A/1	____ @ ____ KG
3	squat	2/A/1	____ @ ____ KG
4	**squat**	2/A/1	____ @ ____ KG
1	dip	2/A/1	____ @ ____ KG
2	dip	2/A/1	____ @ ____ KG
3	dip	2/A/1	____ @ ____ KG
4	**dip**	2/A/1	____ @ ____ KG
1	overhead press	2/A/1	____ @ ____ KG
2	overhead press	2/A/1	____ @ ____ KG
3	overhead press	2/A/1	____ @ ____ KG
4	**overhead press**	2/A/1	____ @ ____ KG
1	push-up	2/A/1	____ @ ____ KG
2	push-up	2/A/1	____ @ ____ KG
3	push-up	2/A/1	____ @ ____ KG
4	**push-up**	2/A/1	____ @ ____ KG

#1 *Do not to train to failure on „non-testing-days".*

#2 *Do not exercise to complete exhaustion either.*

Recovery **Day 31**   R-HR___energy: -

guidelines / what and how to do it:

Probably the best thing to do now is the traditional thai-massage.

If a massage is not availabe, do the joint-mobility-routine.

If you have any muscle-pain, then press the painful point with a foamroller or tennis- / lacrosse-ball for 3 minutes (or more) on it and move on it very slowly.

If you like to do some „sports", or if you have to work physically, then try to stay in „light avtivity".

Remember:

#1 Your heartrate has to stay low, your muscles should not work hard and your passive structures must not be stretched.

#2   keep heart rate lower than BPM: 160-(your age)=_____

#3 If you exercise without a HR-monitor, then do not go harder than you can handle while breathing through your nose. It must feel light / easy to maintain the activity.

#4 Take a look at your rest-heart-rate:

>5 BPM more than normal? Take it easy!

>10 BPM more than normal? You need more than one day for recovery!

Pulling-strength   **Day 32**   R-HR___energy: +++

guidelines / what and how to do it:

Exercise-speed: fast (controlled)   Breaks: 3 to 10 minutes

Set	weight	reps
1	multiply your 1RM by 0,5	5
2	multiply your 1RM by 0,6	5
3	multiply your 1RM by 0,7	5
4	multiply your 1RM by 0,88	3-4

Set	exercise	progr.	Result, reps / weight	calc. 1RM*
1	deadlift	2/A/1	____ @ ____ KG	
2	deadlift	2/A/1	____ @ ____ KG	
3	deadlift	2/A/1	____ @ ____ KG	
4	**deadlift**	2/A/1	____ @ ____ KG	
1	pull-up	2/A/1	____ @ ____ KG	
2	pull-up	2/A/1	____ @ ____ KG	
3	pull-up	2/A/1	____ @ ____ KG	
4	**pull-up**	2/A/1	____ @ ____ KG	
1	hang clean	2/A/1	____ @ ____ KG	
2	hang clean	2/A/1	____ @ ____ KG	
3	hang clean	2/A/1	____ @ ____ KG	
4	**hang clean**	2/A/1	____ @ ____ KG	
1	body row	2/A/1	____ @ ____ KG	
2	body row	2/A/1	____ @ ____ KG	
3	body row	2/A/1	____ @ ____ KG	
4	**body row**	2/A/1	____ @ ____ KG	

#1 *Do not to train to failure on „non-testing-days".*

#2 *Do not exercise to complete exhaustion either.*

Recovery `Day 33`   R-HR___energy: -

<u>*guidelines / what and how to do it:*</u>

Probably the best thing to do now is the traditional thai-massage.

If a massage is not availabe, do the joint-mobility-routine.

If you have any muscle-pain, then press the painful point with a foamroller or tennis- / lacrosse-ball for 3 minutes (or more) on it and move on it very slowly.

If you like to do some „sports", or if you have to work physically, then try to stay in „light avtivity".

Remember:

#1 Your heartrate has to stay low, your muscles should not work hard and your passive structures must not be stretched.

#2 keep heart rate lower than BPM: 160-(your age)=_____

#3 If you exercise without a HR-monitor, then do not go harder than you can handle while breathing through your nose. It must feel light / easy to maintain the activity.

#4 Take a look at your rest-heart-rate:
>5 BPM more than normal? Take it easy!
>10 BPM more than normal? You need more than one day for recovery!

Pushing-endurance   **Day 34**   **R-HR___energy: +**
cardio, 30-90 minutes @ 180 (-age) BPM

<u>*guidelines / what and how to do it:*</u>

Any pushing-activity that you can continue for more than
5 minutes without any rest is O.K. You can also change the
activities after some minutes.

Good examples are jogging, cycling, dancing or shadow-boxing.
Since these activities (except of shadow-boxing)
do not target the upper body, do some moderate paced push-ups
before, after or in between these activities.

Exercise for 30-90 minutes without any rest.
Try to stay constantly at your target-HR.
Move in a loose way.
Breathe in - fill your lungs *completely*.
Breathe out - empty your lungs *completely*.

<u>*Remember:*</u>
- #1 *When ever possible, wear a heartrate-monitor.*
- #2 *target heart rate in BPM: 180-(your age)=_____*
- #3 *If you exercise without a HR-monitor, then do not go harder than you can handle while breathing through your nose.*
- #4 *take longer rests if #2 or #3 is not possible.*

Pulling-endurance　**Day 35**　R-HR___energy:　+
cardio, 30-90 minutes @ 180 (-age) BPM

guidelines / what and how to do it:

Any pulling-activity that you can continue for more than
5 minutes without any rest is O.K. You can also change the
activities after some minutes.

Good examples are swimming, rowing, climbing and ski run long.

Exercise for 30-90 minutes without any rest.
Try to stay constantly at your target-HR.
Move in a loose way.
Breathe in - fill your lungs *completely*.
Breathe out - empty your lungs *completely*.

Remember:

#1 When ever possible, wear a heartrate-monitor.

#2　target heart rate in BPM: 180-(your age)=_____

#3 If you exercise without a HR-monitor, then do not go harder than you can handle while breathing through your nose.

#4 take longer rests if #2 or #3 is not possible.

Flexibility-training **Day 36** R-HR____ energy: +

The best choice is a „hot-yoga-class". No yoga-class available?

A good yoga-video-instructional can help to „do it right".

No yoga-class or video available? No problem! Do this:

Remember:

#1 Listen to your body – „pain" means „Stop! Too much!"

#2 Warm up your body passively before stretching.

#3 Wear warm clothes or heat your room for staying warm.

#4 Support your stretching with proper breathing:

Hold position > breathe in > simultaneously breath out and go deeper into the position > hold position > simultaneousl breath out and go deeper into the position > repeat slowly

target:	the backside of your body
to do:	Do different „forward-bending-exercises".
example:	Lay your back on the floor. Walk your feet slowly clockwise in a big circle around your body far over your head. Repeat the same thing counterclockwise.
target:	the frontside of your body
to do:	Do different „backward-bending-exercises".
example:	Lay your back on a exercise ball and touch the floor over your head, while your feet stay also on the floor. Walk your hands as close as possible in direction to your feet. Bridge as high as possible and hold >20 sec.
target:	your trunk, your hips and your glutes
to do:	Do different „twisting- and splitting exercises".
example:	Do the Triangle Pose „Trikonasana". Do the Half Spinal Twist Pose „Ardha Matsyendrasana' Do front- and side-splits.

Pushing-strength　**Day 37**　R-HR____　test ++++

guidelines / what and how to do it:

Exercise-speed: fast (controlled)　　Breaks: 3 to 10 minutes

Set	weight	reps
1	multiply your last 1RM with 0,6	5
2	multiply your last 1RM with 0,7	5
3	multiply your last 1RM with 0,8	3
4	multiply your last 1RM with 0,9	amrap*

amrap = as many reps as possible

Set	exercise	progr.	Result, reps / weight	calc. 1RM*
1	squat	2/A/1	____ @ ____ KG	
2	squat	2/A/1	____ @ ____ KG	
3	squat	2/A/1	____ @ ____ KG	
4	**squat**	2/A/1	____ @ ____ KG	_____**KG**
1	dip	2/A/1	____ @ ____ KG	
2	dip	2/A/1	____ @ ____ KG	
3	dip	2/A/1	____ @ ____ KG	
4	**dip**	2/A/1	____ @ ____ KG	_____**KG**
1	overhead press	2/A/1	____ @ ____ KG	
2	overhead press	2/A/1	____ @ ____ KG	
3	overhead press	2/A/1	____ @ ____ KG	
4	**overhead press**	2/A/1	____ @ ____ KG	_____**KG**
1	push-up	2/A/1	____ @ ____ KG	
2	push-up	2/A/1	____ @ ____ KG	
3	push-up	2/A/1	____ @ ____ KG	
4	**push-up**	2/A/1	____ @ ____ KG	_____**KG**

Recovery **Day 38**   **R-HR**____   **energy:**   -

guidelines / what and how to do it:

Probably the best thing to do now is the traditional thai-massage.

If a massage is not availabe, do the joint-mobility-routine.

If you have any muscle-pain, then press the painful point with a foamroller or tennis- / lacrosse-ball for 3 minutes (or more) on it and move on it very slowly.

If you like to do some „sports", or if you have to work physically, then try to stay in „light avtivity".

Remember:

#1 Your heartrate has to stay low, your muscles should not work hard and your passive structures must not be stretched.

#2   keep heart rate lower than BPM: 160-(your age)=_____

#3 If you exercise without a HR-monitor, then do not go harder than you can handle while breathing through your nose. It must feel light / easy to maintain the activity.

#4 Take a look at your rest-heart-rate:

>5 BPM more than normal? Take it easy!

>10 BPM more than normal? You need more than one day for recovery!

Pulling-strength　　**Day 39**　　R-HR____　　test ++++

guidelines / what and how to do it:

Exercise-speed: fast (controlled)　　Breaks: 3 to 10 minutes

Set	weight	reps
1	multiply your last 1RM with 0,6	5
2	multiply your last 1RM with 0,7	5
3	multiply your last 1RM with 0,8	3
4	multiply your last 1RM with 0,9	amrap*

amrap = as many reps as possible

Set	exercise	progr.	Result, reps / weight	calc. 1RM*
1	deadlift	2/A/1	____ @ ____ KG	
2	deadlift	2/A/1	____ @ ____ KG	
3	deadlift	2/A/1	____ @ ____ KG	
4	**deadlift**	2/A/1	____ @ ____ KG	____**KG**
1	pull-up	2/A/1	____ @ ____ KG	
2	pull-up	2/A/1	____ @ ____ KG	
3	pull-up	2/A/1	____ @ ____ KG	
4	**pull-up**	2/A/1	____ @ ____ KG	____**KG**
1	hang clean	2/A/1	____ @ ____ KG	
2	hang clean	2/A/1	____ @ ____ KG	
3	hang clean	2/A/1	____ @ ____ KG	
4	**hang clean**	2/A/1	____ @ ____ KG	____**KG**
1	body row	2/A/1	____ @ ____ KG	
2	body row	2/A/1	____ @ ____ KG	
3	body row	2/A/1	____ @ ____ KG	
4	**body row**	2/A/1	____ @ ____ KG	____**KG**

Recovery   **Day 40**   R-HR___ energy: -

<u>guidelines / what and how to do it:</u>

Probably the best thing to do now is the traditional thai-massage.

If a massage is not availabe, do the joint-mobility-routine.

If you have any muscle-pain, then press the painful point
with a foamroller or tennis- / lacrosse-ball for 3 minutes
(or more) on it and move on it very slowly.

If you like to do some „sports", or if you have to work
physically, then try to stay in „light avtivity".

<u>*Remember:*</u>

#1 Your heartrate has to stay low, your muscles should not
    work hard and your passive structures must not be stretched.

#2 keep heart rate lower than BPM: 160-(your age)=_____

#3 If you exercise without a HR-monitor, then do not go
    harder than you can handle while breathing through your
    nose. It must feel light / easy to maintain the activity.

#4 Take a look at your rest-heart-rate:
    >5 BPM more than normal? Take it easy!
    >10 BPM more than normal? You need more than one
    day for recovery!

Pushing-endurance   **Day 41**   R-HR___energy: -

30 to 90 minutes light activities.

Possible activities are jogging, cycling, dancing, shadow-boxing, Rope-skipping and any sports using the arobic energy-system.

Remember:

#1 When ever possible, wear a heartrate-monitor.

#2   keep heart rate in BPM: 160-(your age)=_____

#3 If you exercise without a HR-monitor, then do not go harder than you can handle while breathing through your nose. It must feel light / easy to maintain the activity.

Pulling-endurance   `Day 42`   R-HR___energy: -

30 to 90 minutes light activities.

Possible activities are swimming, rowing, climbing, ski-long-run and any sports using the arobic energy-system.

Remember:

#1 When ever possible, wear a heartrate-monitor.

#2 keep heart rate in BPM: 160-(your age)=_____

#3 If you exercise without a HR-monitor, then do not go harder than you can handle while breathing through your nose. It must feel light / easy to maintain the activity.

Flexibility-training   **Day 43**   R-HR___energy: +

The best choice is a „hot-yoga-class". No yoga-class available?

A good yoga-video-instructional can help to „do it right".

No yoga-class or video available? No problem! Do this:

Remember:

#1 Listen to your body – „pain" means „Stop! Too much!"

#2 Warm up your body passively before stretching.

#3 Wear warm clothes or heat your room for staying warm.

#4 Support your stretching with proper breathing:

Hold position > breathe in > simultaneously breath out and go deeper into the position > hold position > simultaneousl breath out and go deeper into the position > repeat slowly

target: the backside of your body

to do: Do different „forward-bending-exercises".

example: Lay your back on the floor. Walk your feet slowly clockwise in a big circle around your body far over your head. Repeat the same thing counterclockwise.

target: the frontside of your body

to do: Do different „backward-bending-exercises".

example: Lay your back on a exercise ball and touch the floor over your head, while your feet stay also on the floor. Walk your hands as close as possible in direction to your feet. Bridge as high as possible and hold >20 sec.

target: your trunk, your hips and your glutes

to do: Do different „twisting- and splitting exercises".

example: Do the Triangle Pose „Trikonasana".

Do the Half Spinal Twist Pose „Ardha Matsyendrasana'

Do front- and side-splits.

Pushing-strength **Day 44** R-HR___energy: -

guidelines / what and how to do it:

Exercise-speed: moderate   Breaks: 3 to 10 minutes

Set	weight	reps
1	multiply your 1RM by 0,5	5
2	multiply your 1RM by 0,6	5
3	multiply your 1RM by 0,7	5

Set	exercise	progr.	Result, reps / weight	calc. 1RM*
1	squat	2/A/1	____ @ ____ KG	
2	squat	2/A/1	____ @ ____ KG	
3	squat	2/A/1	____ @ ____ KG	
1	dip	2/A/1	____ @ ____ KG	
2	dip	2/A/1	____ @ ____ KG	
3	dip	2/A/1	____ @ ____ KG	
1	overhead press	2/A/1	____ @ ____ KG	
2	overhead press	2/A/1	____ @ ____ KG	
3	overhead press	2/A/1	____ @ ____ KG	
1	push-up	2/A/1	____ @ ____ KG	
2	push-up	2/A/1	____ @ ____ KG	
3	push-up	2/A/1	____ @ ____ KG	

Recovery `Day 45` R-HR___energy: -

guidelines / what and how to do it:

Probably the best thing to do now is the traditional thai-massage.

If a massage is not availabe, do the joint-mobility-routine.

If you have any muscle-pain, then press the painful point with a foamroller or tennis- / lacrosse-ball for 3 minutes (or more) on it and move on it very slowly.

If you like to do some „sports", or if you have to work physically, then try to stay in „light avtivity".

Remember:

#1 Your heartrate has to stay low, your muscles should not work hard and your passive structures must not be stretched.

#2 keep heart rate lower than BPM: 160-(your age)=_____

#3 If you exercise without a HR-monitor, then do not go harder than you can handle while breathing through your nose. It must feel light / easy to maintain the activity.

#4 Take a look at your rest-heart-rate:

>5 BPM more than normal? Take it easy!

>10 BPM more than normal? You need more than one day for recovery!

Pulling-strength   **Day 46**   R-HR____energy: -

guidelines / what and how to do it:

Exercise-speed: moderate   Breaks: 3 to 10 minutes

Set	weight	reps
1	multiply your 1RM by 0,5	5
2	multiply your 1RM by 0,6	5
3	multiply your 1RM by 0,7	5

Set	exercise	progr.	Result, reps / weight	calc. 1RM*
1	deadlift	2/A/1	____ @ ____ KG	
2	deadlift	2/A/1	____ @ ____ KG	
3	deadlift	2/A/1	____ @ ____ KG	
1	pull-up	2/A/1	____ @ ____ KG	
2	pull-up	2/A/1	____ @ ____ KG	
3	pull-up	2/A/1	____ @ ____ KG	
1	hang clean	2/A/1	____ @ ____ KG	
2	hang clean	2/A/1	____ @ ____ KG	
3	hang clean	2/A/1	____ @ ____ KG	
1	body row	2/A/1	____ @ ____ KG	
2	body row	2/A/1	____ @ ____ KG	
3	body row	2/A/1	____ @ ____ KG	

Recovery   **Day 47**   R-HR___energy: -

<u>*guidelines / what and how to do it:*</u>
Probably the best thing to do now is the traditional thai-massage.

If a massage is not availabe, do the joint-mobility-routine.

If you have any muscle-pain, then press the painful point
with a foamroller or tennis- / lacrosse-ball for 3 minutes
(or more) on it and move on it very slowly.

If you like to do some „sports", or if you have to work
physically, then try to stay in „light avtivity".

Remember:

#1 Your heartrate has to stay low, your muscles should not
    work hard and your passive structures must not be stretched.

#2 keep heart rate lower than BPM: 160-(your age)=_____

#3 If you exercise without a HR-monitor, then do not go
    harder than you can handle while breathing through your
    nose. It must feel light / easy to maintain the activity.

#4 Take a look at your rest-heart-rate:
    >5 BPM more than normal? Take it easy!
    >10 BPM more than normal? You need more than one
    day for recovery!

Pushing-endurance   `Day 48`   R-HR____   Test ++++

To test your *lower-body-endurance*, do the "12 Minute Run".

Your target should be 2500 m, or better more than that.

Rest for as long as possible (if possible more than 10 minutes).

To test your upper-body-pushing-endurance, do the "push-up-test'

Your target should be 50 reps in a row, or better more than that.

Track your progress!

Remember:

#1 *When ever possible, wear a heartrate-monitor.*

#2 *target heart rate in BPM: 180-(your age)=_____*

#3 If you exercise without a HR-monitor, then do not go harder than you can handle while breathing through your *nose.*

#4 Testing your strenght in a state of exhaustion can lead to serious injuries.

#5 Be careful with previous activities.

#6 Do not mix strength and endurance tests.

#7 Testing is not competition. Health and safety first!

your score: 12-min-run   ____ m

push-ups   ____ reps

Pulling-endurance   **Day 49**   **R-HR___**   **Test ++++**

To test your upper-body-pulling-endurance, do the "pull-up-test".
Your target should be 20 reps in a row, or better more than that.

Track your progress!

Remember:
#1 Testing your strenght in a state of exhaustion can lead to serious injuries.
#2 Be careful with previous activities.
#3 Do not mix strength and endurance tests.
#4 Testing is not competition. Health and safety first!

your score: pull-ups   ____ reps

Flexibility-training **Day 50** **R-HR___energy: +**

The best choice is a „hot-yoga-class". No yoga-class available?
A good yoga-video-instructional can help to „do it right".
No yoga-class or video available? No problem! Do this:

Remember:
#1 Listen to your body – „pain" means „Stop! Too much!"
#2 Warm up your body passively before stretching.
#3 Wear warm clothes or heat your room for staying warm.
#4 Support your stretching with proper breathing:
Hold position > breathe in > simultaneously breath out and go deeper into the position > hold position > simultaneousl breath out and go deeper into the position > repeat slowly

target: the backside of your body
to do: Do different „forward-bending-exercises".
example: Lay your back on the floor. Walk your feet slowly clockwise in a big circle around your body far over your head. Repeat the same thing counterclockwise.

target: the frontside of your body
to do: Do different „backward-bending-exercises".
example: Lay your back on a exercise ball and touch the floor over your head, while your feet stay also on the floor. Walk your hands as close as possible in direction to your feet. Bridge as high as possible and hold >20 sec.

target: your trunk, your hips and your glutes
to do: Do different „twisting- and splitting exercises".
example: Do the Triangle Pose „Trikonasana".
Do the Half Spinal Twist Pose „Ardha Matsyendrasana'
Do front- and side-splits.

Pushing-strength `Day 51` **R-HR___energy:** +

guidelines / what and how to do it:

Exercise-speed: fast (controlled)   Breaks: 3 to 10 minutes

Set	weight	reps
1	multiply your 1RM by 0,5	5
2	multiply your 1RM by 0,6	5
3	multiply your 1RM by 0,7	5
4	multiply your 1RM by 0,83	5

Set	exercise	progr.	Result, reps / weight
1	squat	2/A/1	____ @ ____ KG
2	squat	2/A/1	____ @ ____ KG
3	squat	2/A/1	____ @ ____ KG
4	**squat**	2/A/1	____ @ ____ KG
1	dip	2/A/1	____ @ ____ KG
2	dip	2/A/1	____ @ ____ KG
3	dip	2/A/1	____ @ ____ KG
4	**dip**	2/A/1	____ @ ____ KG
1	overhead press	2/A/1	____ @ ____ KG
2	overhead press	2/A/1	____ @ ____ KG
3	overhead press	2/A/1	____ @ ____ KG
4	**overhead press**	2/A/1	____ @ ____ KG
1	push-up	2/A/1	____ @ ____ KG
2	push-up	2/A/1	____ @ ____ KG
3	push-up	2/A/1	____ @ ____ KG
4	**push-up**	2/A/1	____ @ ____ KG

Recovery   **Day 52**   R-HR___energy: -

guidelines / what and how to do it:
Probably the best thing to do now is the traditional thai-massage.

If a massage is not availabe, do the joint-mobility-routine.

If you have any muscle-pain, then press the painful point
with a foamroller or tennis- / lacrosse-ball for 3 minutes
(or more) on it and move on it very slowly.

If you like to do some „sports", or if you have to work
physically, then try to stay in „light avtivity".

Remember:
#1 Your heartrate has to stay low, your muscles should not
     work hard and your passive structures must not be stretched.
#2 keep heart rate lower than BPM: 160-(your age)=_____
#3 If you exercise without a HR-monitor, then do not go
     harder than you can handle while breathing through your
     nose. It must feel light / easy to maintain the activity.
#4 Take a look at your rest-heart-rate:
     >5 BPM more than normal? Take it easy!
     >10 BPM more than normal? You need more than one
     day for recovery!

Pulling-strength **Day 53** R-HR___ energy: +

guidelines / what and how to do it:

Exercise-speed: fast (controlled)   Breaks: 3 to 10 minutes

Set	weight	reps
1	multiply your 1RM by 0,5	5
2	multiply your 1RM by 0,6	5
3	multiply your 1RM by 0,7	5
4	multiply your 1RM by 0,83	5

Set	exercise	progr.	Result, reps / weight	calc. 1RM*
1	deadlift	2/A/1	____ @ ____ KG	
2	deadlift	2/A/1	____ @ ____ KG	
3	deadlift	2/A/1	____ @ ____ KG	
4	**deadlift**	2/A/1	____ @ ____ KG	
1	pull-up	2/A/1	____ @ ____ KG	
2	pull-up	2/A/1	____ @ ____ KG	
3	pull-up	2/A/1	____ @ ____ KG	
4	**pull-up**	2/A/1	____ @ ____ KG	
1	hang clean	2/A/1	____ @ ____ KG	
2	hang clean	2/A/1	____ @ ____ KG	
3	hang clean	2/A/1	____ @ ____ KG	
4	**hang clean**	2/A/1	____ @ ____ KG	
1	body row	2/A/1	____ @ ____ KG	
2	body row	2/A/1	____ @ ____ KG	
3	body row	2/A/1	____ @ ____ KG	
4	**body row**	2/A/1	____ @ ____ KG	

Recovery — Day 54 — R-HR___ energy: -

guidelines / what and how to do it:

Probably the best thing to do now is the traditional thai-massage.

If a massage is not availabe, do the joint-mobility-routine.

If you have any muscle-pain, then press the painful point
with a foamroller or tennis- / lacrosse-ball for 3 minutes
(or more) on it and move on it very slowly.

If you like to do some „sports", or if you have to work
physically, then try to stay in „light avtivity".

Remember:

#1 Your heartrate has to stay low, your muscles should not work hard and your passive structures must not be stretched.

#2 keep heart rate lower than BPM: 160-(your age)=_____

#3 If you exercise without a HR-monitor, then do not go harder than you can handle while breathing through your nose. It must feel light / easy to maintain the activity.

#4 Take a look at your rest-heart-rate:

>5 BPM more than normal? Take it easy!

>10 BPM more than normal? You need more than one day for recovery!

Pushing-endurance `Day 55` **R-HR___energy: +++**
intervals, short bursts with short active rests

guidelines / what and how to do it:

If you have access to a heavy punching-bag (or better a training-partner with pads), the best option ist to do punching and kicking. No bag and no partner? Very good activities are burpees, rope-skipping, sprinting and cycling.

Since these activities (except of burpees) do not target the upper body, do explosive push-ups after a 3-10 min rest.

To do these intervals effectively, alternate between short burst of explosive power-movements and slow / easy paced activity.

Set your interval-timer: **rounds= 10-20**

Round-length= 15 sec

active rest= 15 sec

During the round: go hard and fast!
During the active rest: move in a loose way and breathe!

Remember:

#1 *When ever possible, wear a heartrate-monitor.*

#2 *target heart rate in BPM: 180-(your age)=_____*

#3 *If you exercise without a HR-monitor, then do not go harder than you can handle while breathing through your nose.*

#4 *take longer rests if #2 or #3 is not possible.*

Pulling-endurance `Day 56` **R-HR___energy: +++**

intervals, short bursts with short active rests

guidelines / what and how to do it:

Very good activities for this kind of training are swimming, rowing, climbing (ropes), pull-ups, heavy ropes, ski run long and Kettlebell-snatches.

To do these intervals effectively, alternate between short burst of explosive power-movements and slow / easy paced activity.

Set your interval-timer: rounds= 10-20
Round-length= 15 sec
active rest= 15 sec

During the round: go hard and fast!
During the active rest: move in a loose way and breathe!

Remember:
#1 When ever possible, wear a heartrate-monitor.
#2   target heart rate in BPM: 180-(your age)=_____
#3 If you exercise without a HR-monitor, then do not go harder than you can handle while breathing through your nose.
#4 take longer rests if #2 or #3 is not possible.

Flexibility-training　　　**Day 57**　　R-HR___energy:　　　+

The best choice is a „hot-yoga-class". No yoga-class available?

A good yoga-video-instructional can help to „do it right".

No yoga-class or video available? No problem! Do this:

Remember:

#1 Listen to your body – „pain" means „Stop! Too much!"

#2 Warm up your body passively before stretching.

#3 Wear warm clothes or heat your room for staying warm.

#4 Support your stretching with proper breathing:

Hold position > breathe in > simultaneously breath out and go deeper into the position > hold position > simultaneously breath out and go deeper into the position > repeat slowly

target:	the backside of your body

to do:　　Do different „forward-bending-exercises".

example: Lay your back on the floor. Walk your feet slowly clockwise in a big circle around your body far over your head. Repeat the same thing counterclockwise.

target:	the frontside of your body

to do:　　Do different „backward-bending-exercises".

example: Lay your back on a exercise ball and touch the floor over your head, while your feet stay also on the floor. Walk your hands as close as possible in direction to your feet. Bridge as high as possible and hold >20 sec.

target:	your trunk, your hips and your glutes

to do:　　Do different „twisting- and splitting exercises".

example: Do the Triangle Pose „Trikonasana".

　　　　　　Do the Half Spinal Twist Pose „Ardha Matsyendrasana"

　　　　　　Do front- and side-splits.

Pushing-strength **Day 58** **R-HR___energy:** ++

guidelines / what and how to do it:

Exercise-speed: fast (controlled)   Breaks: 3 to 10 minutes

Set	weight	reps
1	multiply your 1RM by 0,5	5
2	multiply your 1RM by 0,6	5
3	multiply your 1RM by 0,7	5
4	multiply your 1RM by 0,86	3-4

Set	exercise	progr.	Result, reps / weight
1	squat	2/A/1	____ @ ____ KG
2	squat	2/A/1	____ @ ____ KG
3	squat	2/A/1	____ @ ____ KG
4	**squat**	2/A/1	____ @ ____ KG
1	dip	2/A/1	____ @ ____ KG
2	dip	2/A/1	____ @ ____ KG
3	dip	2/A/1	____ @ ____ KG
4	**dip**	2/A/1	____ @ ____ KG
1	overhead press	2/A/1	____ @ ____ KG
2	overhead press	2/A/1	____ @ ____ KG
3	overhead press	2/A/1	____ @ ____ KG
4	**overhead press**	2/A/1	____ @ ____ KG
1	push-up	2/A/1	____ @ ____ KG
2	push-up	2/A/1	____ @ ____ KG
3	push-up	2/A/1	____ @ ____ KG
4	**push-up**	2/A/1	____ @ ____ KG

#1 *Do not to train to failure on „non-testing-days".*

#2 *Do not exercise to complete exhaustion either.*

Recovery **Day 59** R-HR___ energy: -

guidelines / what and how to do it:
Probably the best thing to do now is the traditional thai-massage.

If a massage is not availabe, do the joint-mobility-routine.

If you have any muscle-pain, then press the painful point with a foamroller or tennis- / lacrosse-ball for 3 minutes (or more) on it and move on it very slowly.

If you like to do some „sports", or if you have to work physically, then try to stay in „light avtivity".

Remember:

#1 Your heartrate has to stay low, your muscles should not work hard and your passive structures must not be stretched.

#2 keep heart rate lower than BPM: 160-(your age)=_____

#3 If you exercise without a HR-monitor, then do not go harder than you can handle while breathing through your nose. It must feel light / easy to maintain the activity.

#4 Take a look at your rest-heart-rate:
>5 BPM more than normal? Take it easy!
>10 BPM more than normal? You need more than one day for recovery!

Pulling-strength　**Day 60**　**R-HR___energy:**　++

guidelines / what and how to do it:

Exercise-speed: fast (controlled)　　Breaks: 3 to 10 minutes

Set	weight	reps
1	multiply your 1RM by 0,5	5
2	multiply your 1RM by 0,6	5
3	multiply your 1RM by 0,7	5
4	multiply your 1RM by 0,86	3-4

Set	exercise	progr.	Result, reps / weight	calc. 1RM*
1	deadlift	2/A/1	____ @ ____ KG	
2	deadlift	2/A/1	____ @ ____ KG	
3	deadlift	2/A/1	____ @ ____ KG	
4	**deadlift**	2/A/1	____ @ ____ KG	
1	pull-up	2/A/1	____ @ ____ KG	
2	pull-up	2/A/1	____ @ ____ KG	
3	pull-up	2/A/1	____ @ ____ KG	
4	**pull-up**	2/A/1	____ @ ____ KG	
1	hang clean	2/A/1	____ @ ____ KG	
2	hang clean	2/A/1	____ @ ____ KG	
3	hang clean	2/A/1	____ @ ____ KG	
4	**hang clean**	2/A/1	____ @ ____ KG	
1	body row	2/A/1	____ @ ____ KG	
2	body row	2/A/1	____ @ ____ KG	
3	body row	2/A/1	____ @ ____ KG	
4	**body row**	2/A/1	____ @ ____ KG	

#1 *Do not to train to failure on „non-testing-days".*

#2 *Do not exercise to complete exhaustion either.*

Recovery **Day 61** **R-HR___energy: -**

guidelines / what and how to do it:

Probably the best thing to do now is the traditional thai-massage.

If a massage is not availabe, do the joint-mobility-routine.

If you have any muscle-pain, then press the painful point with a foamroller or tennis- / lacrosse-ball for 3 minutes (or more) on it and move on it very slowly.

If you like to do some „sports", or if you have to work physically, then try to stay in „light avtivity".

Remember:

#1 Your heartrate has to stay low, your muscles should not work hard and your passive structures must not be stretched.

#2 keep heart rate lower than BPM: 160-(your age)=_____

#3 If you exercise without a HR-monitor, then do not go harder than you can handle while breathing through your nose. It must feel light / easy to maintain the activity.

#4 Take a look at your rest-heart-rate:

>5 BPM more than normal? Take it easy!

>10 BPM more than normal? You need more than one day for recovery!

Pushing-endurance   **Day 62**   **R-HR___energy: ++**

intervals, short bursts with long active rests

guidelines / what and how to do it:

If you have access to a heavy punching-bag (or better a training-partner with pads), the best option ist to do punching and kicking. No bag and no partner? Very good activities are burpees, rope-skipping, sprinting and cycling.

Since these activities (except of burpees) do not target the upper body, do explosive push-ups after a 3-10 min rest.

To do these intervals effectively, alternate between short burst of explosive power-movements and slow / easy paced activity.

Set your interval-timer: **rounds= 10-20**

Round-length= 10 sec

active rest= 40-90 sec

During the round: go hard and fast!
During the active rest: move in a loose way and breathe!

Remember:

#1 *When ever possible, wear a heartrate-monitor.*

#2 *target heart rate in BPM: 180-(your age)=_____*

#3 *If you exercise without a HR-monitor, then do not go harder than you can handle while breathing through your nose.*

#4 *take longer rests if #2 or #3 is not possible.*

Pulling-endurance　　**Day 63**　　**R-HR___energy:**　　**++**
intervals, short bursts with long active rests

guidelines / what and how to do it:

Very good activities for this kind of training are swimming, rowing, climbing (ropes), pull-ups, heavy ropes, ski run long and Kettlebell-snatches.

To do these intervals effectively, alternate between short burst of explosive power-movements and slow / easy paced activity.

Set your interval-timer:　　　　**rounds= 10-20**
Round-length= 10 sec
active rest= 40-90 sec

During the round: go hard and fast!
During the active rest: move in a loose way and breathe!

Remember:

#1 *When ever possible, wear a heartrate-monitor.*

#2 *target heart rate in BPM: 180-(your age)=_____*

#3 *If you exercise without a HR-monitor, then do not go harder than you can handle while breathing through your nose.*

#4 *take longer rests if #2 or #3 is not possible.*

Flexibility-training   `Day 64`   R-HR___energy: +

The best choice is a „hot-yoga-class". No yoga-class available?
A good yoga-video-instructional can help to „do it right".
No yoga-class or video available? No problem! Do this:

Remember:

#1 Listen to your body – „pain" means „Stop! Too much!"

#2 Warm up your body passively before stretching.

#3 Wear warm clothes or heat your room for staying warm.

#4 Support your stretching with proper breathing:

Hold position > breathe in > simultaneously breath out and go deeper into the position > hold position > simultaneousl breath out and go deeper into the position > repeat slowly

target: the backside of your body

to do: Do different „forward-bending-exercises".

example: Lay your back on the floor. Walk your feet slowly clockwise in a big circle around your body far over your head. Repeat the same thing counterclockwise.

target: the frontside of your body

to do: Do different „backward-bending-exercises".

example: Lay your back on a exercise ball and touch the floor over your head, while your feet stay also on the floor. Walk your hands as close as possible in direction to your feet. Bridge as high as possible and hold >20 sec.

target: your trunk, your hips and your glutes

to do: Do different „twisting- and splitting exercises".

example: Do the Triangle Pose „Trikonasana".
Do the Half Spinal Twist Pose „Ardha Matsyendrasana'
Do front- and side-splits.

Pushing-strength   **Day 65**   **R-HR___ energy: +++**

guidelines / what and how to do it:

Exercise-speed: fast (controlled)   Breaks: 3 to 10 minutes

Set	weight	reps
1	multiply your 1RM by 0,5	5
2	multiply your 1RM by 0,6	5
3	multiply your 1RM by 0,7	5
4	multiply your 1RM by 0,88	3-4

Set	exercise	progr.	Result, reps / weight
1	squat	2/A/1	____ @ ____ KG
2	squat	2/A/1	____ @ ____ KG
3	squat	2/A/1	____ @ ____ KG
4	**squat**	2/A/1	____ @ ____ KG
1	dip	2/A/1	____ @ ____ KG
2	dip	2/A/1	____ @ ____ KG
3	dip	2/A/1	____ @ ____ KG
4	**dip**	2/A/1	____ @ ____ KG
1	overhead press	2/A/1	____ @ ____ KG
2	overhead press	2/A/1	____ @ ____ KG
3	overhead press	2/A/1	____ @ ____ KG
4	**overhead press**	2/A/1	____ @ ____ KG
1	push-up	2/A/1	____ @ ____ KG
2	push-up	2/A/1	____ @ ____ KG
3	push-up	2/A/1	____ @ ____ KG
4	**push-up**	2/A/1	____ @ ____ KG

#1 *Do not to train to failure on „non-testing-days".*

#2 *Do not exercise to complete exhaustion either.*

Recovery — Day 66   R-HR___ energy: -

guidelines / what and how to do it:

Probably the best thing to do now is the traditional thai-massage.

If a massage is not availabe, do the joint-mobility-routine.

If you have any muscle-pain, then press the painful point with a foamroller or tennis- / lacrosse-ball for 3 minutes (or more) on it and move on it very slowly.

If you like to do some „sports", or if you have to work physically, then try to stay in „light avtivity".

Remember:

#1 Your heartrate has to stay low, your muscles should not work hard and your passive structures must not be stretched.

#2 keep heart rate lower than BPM: 160-(your age)=_____

#3 If you exercise without a HR-monitor, then do not go harder than you can handle while breathing through your nose. It must feel light / easy to maintain the activity.

#4 Take a look at your rest-heart-rate:

> >5 BPM more than normal? Take it easy!
> >10 BPM more than normal? You need more than one day for recovery!

Pulling-strength **Day 67** **R-HR___energy: +++**

guidelines / what and how to do it:

Exercise-speed: fast (controlled)   Breaks: 3 to 10 minutes

Set	weight	reps
1	multiply your 1RM by 0,5	5
2	multiply your 1RM by 0,6	5
3	multiply your 1RM by 0,7	5
4	multiply your 1RM by 0,88	3-4

Set	exercise	progr.	Result, reps / weight	calc. 1RM*
1	deadlift	2/A/1	____ @ ____ KG	
2	deadlift	2/A/1	____ @ ____ KG	
3	deadlift	2/A/1	____ @ ____ KG	
4	**deadlift**	2/A/1	____ @ ____ KG	
1	pull-up	2/A/1	____ @ ____ KG	
2	pull-up	2/A/1	____ @ ____ KG	
3	pull-up	2/A/1	____ @ ____ KG	
4	**pull-up**	2/A/1	____ @ ____ KG	
1	hang clean	2/A/1	____ @ ____ KG	
2	hang clean	2/A/1	____ @ ____ KG	
3	hang clean	2/A/1	____ @ ____ KG	
4	**hang clean**	2/A/1	____ @ ____ KG	
1	body row	2/A/1	____ @ ____ KG	
2	body row	2/A/1	____ @ ____ KG	
3	body row	2/A/1	____ @ ____ KG	
4	**body row**	2/A/1	____ @ ____ KG	

#1 *Do not to train to failure on „non-testing-days".*

#2 *Do not exercise to complete exhaustion either.*

Recovery — Day 68 — R-HR___energy: -

guidelines / what and how to do it:

Probably the best thing to do now is the traditional thai-massage.

If a massage is not availabe, do the joint-mobility-routine.

If you have any muscle-pain, then press the painful point with a foamroller or tennis- / lacrosse-ball for 3 minutes (or more) on it and move on it very slowly.

If you like to do some „sports", or if you have to work physically, then try to stay in „light avtivity".

Remember:

#1 Your heartrate has to stay low, your muscles should not work hard and your passive structures must not be stretched.

#2 keep heart rate lower than BPM: 160-(your age)=_____

#3 If you exercise without a HR-monitor, then do not go harder than you can handle while breathing through your nose. It must feel light / easy to maintain the activity.

#4 Take a look at your rest-heart-rate:
>5 BPM more than normal? Take it easy!
>10 BPM more than normal? You need more than one day for recovery!

Pushing-endurance `Day 69` **R-HR___energy: +**

cardio, 30-90 minutes @ 180 (-age) BPM

guidelines / what and how to do it:

Any pushing-activity that you can continue for more than
5 minutes without any rest is O.K. You can also change the
activities after some minutes.

Good examples are jogging, cycling, dancing or shadow-boxing.
Since these activities (except of shadow-boxing)
do not target the upper body, do some moderate paced push-ups
before, after or in between these activities.

Exercise for 30-90 minutes without any rest.
Try to stay constantly at your target-HR.
Move in a loose way.
Breathe in - fill your lungs *completely*.
Breathe out - empty your lungs *completely*.

Remember:

#1 *When ever possible, wear a heartrate-monitor.*

#2 *target heart rate in BPM: 180-(your age)=_____*

#3 *If you exercise without a HR-monitor, then do not go*
harder than you can handle while breathing through your
nose.

#4 *take longer rests if #2 or #3 is not possible.*

Pulling-endurance　**Day 70**　R-HR___energy:　　+
cardio, 30-90 minutes @ 180 (-age) BPM

guidelines / what and how to do it:

Any pulling-activity that you can continue for more than
5 minutes without any rest is O.K. You can also change the
activities after some minutes.

Good examples are swimming, rowing, climbing and ski run long.

Exercise for 30-90 minutes without any rest.
Try to stay constantly at your target-HR.
Move in a loose way.
Breathe in - fill your lungs *completely*.
Breathe out - empty your lungs *completely*.

Remember:

#1 *When ever possible, wear a heartrate-monitor.*

#2 *target heart rate in BPM: 180-(your age)=_____*

#3 *If you exercise without a HR-monitor, then do not go harder than you can handle while breathing through your nose.*

#4 *take longer rests if #2 or #3 is not possible.*

Flexibility-training   `Day 71`   **R-HR___**   **energy: +**

The best choice is a „hot-yoga-class". No yoga-class available? A good yoga-video-instructional can help to „do it right".

No yoga-class or video available? No problem! Do this:

Remember:

#1 Listen to your body – „pain" means „Stop! Too much!"

#2 Warm up your body passively before stretching.

#3 Wear warm clothes or heat your room for staying warm.

#4 Support your stretching with proper breathing:

Hold position > breathe in > simultaneously breath out and go deeper into the position > hold position > simultaneousl[y] breath out and go deeper into the position > repeat slowly

target:	the backside of your body

to do: Do different „forward-bending-exercises".

example: Lay your back on the floor. Walk your feet slowly clockwise in a big circle around your body far over your head. Repeat the same thing counterclockwise.

target:	the frontside of your body

to do: Do different „backward-bending-exercises".

example: Lay your back on a exercise ball and touch the floor over your head, while your feet stay also on the floor. Walk your hands as close as possible in direction to your feet. Bridge as high as possible and hold >20 sec.

target:	your trunk, your hips and your glutes

to do: Do different „twisting- and splitting exercises".

example: Do the Triangle Pose „Trikonasana".

Do the Half Spinal Twist Pose „Ardha Matsyendrasana"

Do front- and side-splits.

Pushing-strength `Day 72` R-HR____ test ++++

guidelines / what and how to do it:

Exercise-speed: fast (controlled)   Breaks: 3 to 10 minutes

Set	weight	reps
1	multiply your last 1RM with 0,6	5
2	multiply your last 1RM with 0,7	5
3	multiply your last 1RM with 0,8	3
4	multiply your last 1RM with 0,9	amrap*

amrap = as many reps as possible

Set	exercise	progr.	Result, reps / weight	calc. 1RM*
1	squat	2/A/1	____ @ ____ KG	
2	squat	2/A/1	____ @ ____ KG	
3	squat	2/A/1	____ @ ____ KG	
4	**squat**	2/A/1	____ @ ____ KG	_____**KG**
1	dip	2/A/1	____ @ ____ KG	
2	dip	2/A/1	____ @ ____ KG	
3	dip	2/A/1	____ @ ____ KG	
4	**dip**	2/A/1	____ @ ____ KG	_____**KG**
1	overhead press	2/A/1	____ @ ____ KG	
2	overhead press	2/A/1	____ @ ____ KG	
3	overhead press	2/A/1	____ @ ____ KG	
4	**overhead press**	2/A/1	____ @ ____ KG	_____**KG**
1	push-up	2/A/1	____ @ ____ KG	
2	push-up	2/A/1	____ @ ____ KG	
3	push-up	2/A/1	____ @ ____ KG	
4	**push-up**	2/A/1	____ @ ____ KG	_____**KG**

Recovery   **Day 73**   R-HR____   energy: -

guidelines / what and how to do it:

Probably the best thing to do now is the traditional thai-massage.

If a massage is not availabe, do the joint-mobility-routine.

If you have any muscle-pain, then press the painful point with a foamroller or tennis- / lacrosse-ball for 3 minutes (or more) on it and move on it very slowly.

If you like to do some „sports", or if you have to work physically, then try to stay in „light avtivity".

Remember:

#1 Your heartrate has to stay low, your muscles should not work hard and your passive structures must not be stretched.

#2 keep heart rate lower than BPM: 160-(your age)=_____

#3 If you exercise without a HR-monitor, then do not go harder than you can handle while breathing through your nose. It must feel light / easy to maintain the activity.

#4 Take a look at your rest-heart-rate:
>5 BPM more than normal? Take it easy!
>10 BPM more than normal? You need more than one day for recovery!

Pulling-strength   **Day 74**   **R-HR___**   **test ++++**

guidelines / what and how to do it:

Exercise-speed: fast (controlled)   Breaks: 3 to 10 minutes

Set	weight	reps
1	multiply your last 1RM with 0,6	5
2	multiply your last 1RM with 0,7	5
3	multiply your last 1RM with 0,8	3
4	multiply your last 1RM with 0,9	amrap*

amrap = as many reps as possible

Set	exercise	progr.	Result, reps / weight	calc. 1RM*
1	deadlift	2/A/1	____ @ ____ KG	
2	deadlift	2/A/1	____ @ ____ KG	
3	deadlift	2/A/1	____ @ ____ KG	
4	**deadlift**	2/A/1	____ @ ____ KG	____**KG**
1	pull-up	2/A/1	____ @ ____ KG	
2	pull-up	2/A/1	____ @ ____ KG	
3	pull-up	2/A/1	____ @ ____ KG	
4	**pull-up**	2/A/1	____ @ ____ KG	____**KG**
1	hang clean	2/A/1	____ @ ____ KG	
2	hang clean	2/A/1	____ @ ____ KG	
3	hang clean	2/A/1	____ @ ____ KG	
4	**hang clean**	2/A/1	____ @ ____ KG	____**KG**
1	body row	2/A/1	____ @ ____ KG	
2	body row	2/A/1	____ @ ____ KG	
3	body row	2/A/1	____ @ ____ KG	
4	**body row**	2/A/1	____ @ ____ KG	____**KG**

Recovery   **Day 75**   **R-HR___energy:**   -

<u>guidelines / what and how to do it:</u>

Probably the best thing to do now is the traditional thai-massage.

If a massage is not availabe, do the joint-mobility-routine.

If you have any muscle-pain, then press the painful point with a foamroller or tennis- / lacrosse-ball for 3 minutes (or more) on it and move on it very slowly.

If you like to do some „sports", or if you have to work physically, then try to stay in „light avtivity".

Remember:

#1 Your heartrate has to stay low, your muscles should not work hard and your passive structures must not be stretched.

#2 keep heart rate lower than BPM: 160-(your age)=_____

#3 If you exercise without a HR-monitor, then do not go harder than you can handle while breathing through your nose. It must feel light / easy to maintain the activity.

#4 Take a look at your rest-heart-rate:
>   >5 BPM more than normal? Take it easy!
>   >10 BPM more than normal? You need more than one day for recovery!

Pushing-endurance   **Day 76**   R-HR___energy: -

30 to 90 minutes light activities.

Possible activities are jogging, cycling, dancing, shadow-boxing, Rope-skipping and any sports using the arobic energy-system.

Remember:

#1 When ever possible, wear a heartrate-monitor.

#2 keep heart rate in BPM: 160-(your age)=_____

#3 If you exercise without a HR-monitor, then do not go harder than you can handle while breathing through your nose. It must feel light / easy to maintain the activity.

Pulling-endurance   **Day 77**   **R-HR___energy:**   -

30 to 90 minutes light activities.

Possible activities are swimming, rowing, climbing, ski-long-run and any sports using the arobic energy-system.

Remember:

#1 When ever possible, wear a heartrate-monitor.

#2 keep heart rate in BPM: 160-(your age)=_____

#3 If you exercise without a HR-monitor, then do not go harder than you can handle while breathing through your nose. It must feel light / easy to maintain the activity.

Flexibility-training 　**Day 78**　　R-HR____　　energy: +

The best choice is a „hot-yoga-class". No yoga-class available? A good yoga-video-instructional can help to „do it right".

No yoga-class or video available? No problem! Do this:

Remember:

#1 Listen to your body – „pain" means „Stop! Too much!"

#2 Warm up your body passively before stretching.

#3 Wear warm clothes or heat your room for staying warm.

#4 Support your stretching with proper breathing:

Hold position > breathe in > simultaneously breath out and go deeper into the position > hold position > simultaneousl breath out and go deeper into the position > repeat slowly

target:	the backside of your body

to do:　　Do different „forward-bending-exercises".

example:　Lay your back on the floor. Walk your feet slowly clockwise in a big circle around your body far over your head. Repeat the same thing counterclockwise.

target:	the frontside of your body

to do:　　Do different „backward-bending-exercises".

example:　Lay your back on a exercise ball and touch the floor over your head, while your feet stay also on the floor. Walk your hands as close as possible in direction to your feet. Bridge as high as possible and hold >20 sec.

target:	your trunk, your hips and your glutes

to do:　　Do different „twisting- and splitting exercises".

example:　Do the Triangle Pose „Trikonasana".

　　　　　　Do the Half Spinal Twist Pose „Ardha Matsyendrasana'

　　　　　　Do front- and side-splits.

Pushing-strength　　**Day 79**　　„plateau-breaker"

guidelines / what and how to do it:　　**R-HR___**

The exercise-speed is **VERY SLOW!** Move slowly without any stoppage. 1 rep (up and down) is about 20 seconds (!)

For each set try about ½ of your max and do 5-10 reps. (amrap)

You are not able to complete 5 reps? Take less for this exercise!

You can complete 11 reps? Take more!

Variety for the different exercises is possible from 10-60% of 1RM!

amrap = as many reps as possible

Set	exercise	progr.	Result, reps / weight	Next week:
1	squat	2/A/1	___ @ ___ KG	O.K / less / more
		3 min active rest*		
2	squat	2/A/1	___ @ ___ KG	O.K / less / more
		3 min active rest*		
3	squat	2/A/1	___ @ ___ KG	O.K / less / more
		3 min active rest*		
4	squat	2/A/1	___ @ ___ KG	O.K / less / more
		3 min active rest*		
1	push-up	2/A/1	___ @ ___ KG	O.K / less / more
		3 min active rest*		
2	push-up	2/A/1	___ @ ___ KG	O.K / less / more
		3 min active rest*		
3	push-up	2/A/1	___ @ ___ KG	O.K / less / more
		3 min active rest*		
4	push-up	2/A/1	___ @ ___ KG	O.K / less / more
		cool down*		

*3 min very light arobic exercise, like jogging, cycling, dancing, shadow-boxing, jumping jacks, step-ups…

Recovery — Day 80   R-HR____   energy: -

guidelines / what and how to do it:

Probably the best thing to do now is the traditional thai-massage.

If a massage is not availabe, do the joint-mobility-routine.

If you have any muscle-pain, then press the painful point with a foamroller or tennis- / lacrosse-ball for 3 minutes (or more) on it and move on it very slowly.

If you like to do some „sports", or if you have to work physically, then try to stay in „light avtivity".

Remember:

#1 Your heartrate has to stay low, your muscles should not work hard and your passive structures must not be stretched.

#2   keep heart rate lower than BPM: 160-(your age)=_____

#3 If you exercise without a HR-monitor, then do not go harder than you can handle while breathing through your nose. It must feel light / easy to maintain the activity.

#4 Take a look at your rest-heart-rate:

>5 BPM more than normal? Take it easy!

>10 BPM more than normal? You need more than one day for recovery!

Pulling-strength   `Day 81`   „plateau-breaker"

guidelines / what and how to do it: **R-HR___**

The exercise-speed is **VERY SLOW!** Move slowly without any stoppage. 1 rep (up and down) is about 20 seconds (!)
For each set try about ½ of your max and do 5-10 reps. (amrap)
You are not able to complete 5 reps? Take less for this exercise!
You can complete 11 reps? Take more!
Variety for the different exercises is possible from 10-60% of 1RM!
*amrap = as many reps as possible

Set	exercise	progr.	Result, reps / weight			*Next week:*
1	deadlift	2/A/1	____	@	____ KG	O.K / less / more
		3 min active rest				
2	deadlift	2/A/1	____	@	____ KG	O.K / less / more
		3 min active rest				
3	deadlift	2/A/1	____	@	____ KG	O.K / less / more
		3 min active rest				
4	deadlift	2/A/1	____	@	____ KG	O.K / less / more
		3 min active rest				
1	pull-up	2/A/1	____	@	____ KG	O.K / less / more
		3 min active rest				
2	pull-up	2/A/1	____	@	____ KG	O.K / less / more
		3 min active rest				
3	pull-up	2/A/1	____	@	____ KG	O.K / less / more
		3 min active rest				
4	pull-up	2/A/1	____	@	____ KG	O.K / less / more
		cool down				

*3 min very light arobic exercise, like rowing, jogging, cycling, dancing, shadow-boxing, …

Recovery Day 82 R-HR___energy: -

guidelines / what and how to do it:

Probably the best thing to do now is the traditional thai-massage.

If a massage is not availabe, do the joint-mobility-routine.

If you have any muscle-pain, then press the painful point with a foamroller or tennis- / lacrosse-ball for 3 minutes (or more) on it and move on it very slowly.

If you like to do some „sports", or if you have to work physically, then try to stay in „light avtivity".

Remember:

#1 Your heartrate has to stay low, your muscles should not work hard and your passive structures must not be stretched.

#2 keep heart rate lower than BPM: 160-(your age)=_____

#3 If you exercise without a HR-monitor, then do not go harder than you can handle while breathing through your nose. It must feel light / easy to maintain the activity.

#4 Take a look at your rest-heart-rate:
>5 BPM more than normal? Take it easy!
>10 BPM more than normal? You need more than one day for recovery!

Pushing-endurance   `Day 83`   **R-HR___ energy: ++++**
„fight pace"

guidelines / what and how to do it:

If you have access to a heavy punching-bag (or better a training-partner with pads), the best option is to do punching and kicking. No bag and no partner? Very good activities are burpees, rope-skipping, running and cycling.

Since these activities (except of burpees) do not target the upper body, do very slow push-ups after a 3-10 min rest.

Go as hard and fast as possible in a tempo, that you can maintain for the complete round.

Set your interval-timer: rounds= 3-5
                                  Round-length= 5 min
                                  rest= 60 sec

The keys to success: **§1 move loose and quick**
                           §2 move in a steady rhythm
                           §3 breathe in the right rhythm

Remember:

#1 When ever possible, wear a heartrate-monitor.

#2 Target HR = average HR of your 12min-run = _____

#3 If you exercise without a HR-monitor, then try to find a pace you can maintain the complete round.

#4 slow down if #2 or #3 is not possible.

Recovery — Day 84   R-HR___ energy: -

guidelines / what and how to do it:

Probably the best thing to do now is the traditional thai-massage.

If a massage is not availabe, do the joint-mobility-routine.

If you have any muscle-pain, then press the painful point with a foamroller or tennis- / lacrosse-ball for 3 minutes (or more) on it and move on it very slowly.

If you like to do some „sports", or if you have to work physically, then try to stay in „light avtivity".

Remember:

#1 Your heartrate has to stay low, your muscles should not work hard and your passive structures must not be stretched.

#2 keep heart rate lower than BPM: 160-(your age)=_____

#3 If you exercise without a HR-monitor, then do not go harder than you can handle while breathing through your nose. It must feel light / easy to maintain the activity.

#4 Take a look at your rest-heart-rate:
>5 BPM more than normal? Take it easy!
>10 BPM more than normal? You need more than one day for recovery!

Flexibility-training **Day 85** **R-HR___** **energy: +**

The best choice is a „hot-yoga-class". No yoga-class available?
A good yoga-video-instructional can help to „do it right".
No yoga-class or video available? No problem! Do this:

Remember:

#1 Listen to your body – „pain" means „Stop! Too much!"

#2 Warm up your body passively before stretching.

#3 Wear warm clothes or heat your room for staying warm.

#4 Support your stretching with proper breathing:

Hold position > breathe in > simultaneously breath out and go deeper into the position > hold position > simultaneousl breath out and go deeper into the position > repeat slowly

target: the backside of your body

to do: Do different „forward-bending-exercises".

example: Lay your back on the floor. Walk your feet slowly clockwise in a big circle around your body far over your head. Repeat the same thing counterclockwise.

target: the frontside of your body

to do: Do different „backward-bending-exercises".

example: Lay your back on a exercise ball and touch the floor over your head, while your feet stay also on the floor. Walk your hands as close as possible in direction to your feet. Bridge as high as possible and hold >20 sec.

target: your trunk, your hips and your glutes

to do: Do different „twisting- and splitting exercises".

example: Do the Triangle Pose „Trikonasana".
Do the Half Spinal Twist Pose „Ardha Matsyendrasana'
Do front- and side-splits.

Pulling-endurance | **Day 86** | R-HR___ energy: ++++

„fight pace"

guidelines / what and how to do it:

Possible activities are swimming, rowing, climbing, ski-long-run, heavy ropes and any sports using the arobic energy-system.

Go as hard and fast as possible in a tempo, that you can maintain for the complete round.

Set your interval-timer: rounds= 3-5

Round-length= 5 min

rest= 60 sec

The keys to success: **§1 move loose and quick**

§2 move in a steady rhythm

§3 breathe in the right rhythm

Remember:

#1 *When ever possible, wear a heartrate-monitor.*

#2 *Target HR = average HR of your 12min-run = _____*

#3 If you exercise without a HR-monitor, then try to find a pace you can maintain the complete round.

#4 slow down if #2 or #3 is not possible.

Recovery **Day 87** **R-HR____   energy: -**

guidelines / what and how to do it:

Probably the best thing to do now is the traditional thai-massage.

If a massage is not availabe, do the joint-mobility-routine.

If you have any muscle-pain, then press the painful point
with a foamroller or tennis- / lacrosse-ball for 3 minutes
(or more) on it and move on it very slowly.

If you like to do some „sports", or if you have to work
physically, then try to stay in „light avtivity".

Remember:

#1 Your heartrate has to stay low, your muscles should not
    work hard and your passive structures must not be stretched.

#2 keep heart rate lower than BPM: 160-(your age)=_____

#3 If you exercise without a HR-monitor, then do not go
    harder than you can handle while breathing through your
    nose. It must feel light / easy to maintain the activity.

#4 Take a look at your rest-heart-rate:
    >5 BPM more than normal? Take it easy!
    >10 BPM more than normal? You need more than one
    day for recovery!

Pulling-strength **Day 88** **R-HR „plateau-breaker"**

guidelines / what and how to do it:

The exercise-speed is **VERY SLOW!** Move slowly without any stoppage. 1 rep (up and down) is about 20 seconds (!)

For each set try about ½ of your max and do 5-10 reps. (amrap)

You are not able to complete 5 reps? Take less for this exercise!

You can complete 11 reps? Take more!

Variety for the different exercises is possible from 10-60% of 1RM!

amrap = as many reps as possible

Set	exercise	progr.	Result, reps / weight			Next week:
1	deadlift	2/A/1	____	@	____ KG	O.K / less / more
		*3 min active rest**				
2	deadlift	2/A/1	____	@	____ KG	O.K / less / more
		*3 min active rest**				
3	deadlift	2/A/1	____	@	____ KG	O.K / less / more
		*3 min active rest**				
4	deadlift	2/A/1	____	@	____ KG	O.K / less / more
		*3 min active rest**				
1	pull-up	2/A/1	____	@	____ KG	O.K / less / more
		*3 min active rest**				
2	pull-up	2/A/1	____	@	____ KG	O.K / less / more
		*3 min active rest**				
3	pull-up	2/A/1	____	@	____ KG	O.K / less / more
		*3 min active rest**				
4	pull-up	2/A/1	____	@	____ KG	O.K / less / more
		*cool down**				

*3 min very light arobic exercise, like rowing, jogging, cycling, dancing, shadow-boxing, …

Recovery `Day 89` R-HR___ energy: -

guidelines / what and how to do it:

Probably the best thing to do now is the traditional thai-massage.

If a massage is not availabe, do the joint-mobility-routine.

If you have any muscle-pain, then press the painful point with a foamroller or tennis- / lacrosse-ball for 3 minutes (or more) on it and move on it very slowly.

If you like to do some „sports", or if you have to work physically, then try to stay in „light avtivity".

Remember:

#1 Your heartrate has to stay low, your muscles should not work hard and your passive structures must not be stretched.

#2 keep heart rate lower than BPM: 160-(your age)=_____

#3 If you exercise without a HR-monitor, then do not go harder than you can handle while breathing through your nose. It must feel light / easy to maintain the activity.

#4 Take a look at your rest-heart-rate:
>5 BPM more than normal? Take it easy!
>10 BPM more than normal? You need more than one day for recovery!

Pulling-strength　　**Day 90**　　**R-HR „plateau-breaker"**

guidelines / what and how to do it:

The exercise-speed is **VERY SLOW!** Move slowly without any stoppage. 1 rep (up and down) is about 20 seconds (!)

For each set try about ½ of your max and do 5-10 reps. (amrap)

You are not able to complete 5 reps? Take less for this exercise!

You can complete 11 reps? Take more!

Variety for the different exercises is possible from 10-60% of 1RM!

amrap = as many reps as possible

Set	exercise	progr.	Result, reps / weight	*Next week:*
1	deadlift	2/A/1	____ @ ____ KG	O.K / less / more
		3 min active rest*		
2	deadlift	2/A/1	____ @ ____ KG	O.K / less / more
		3 min active rest*		
3	deadlift	2/A/1	____ @ ____ KG	O.K / less / more
		3 min active rest*		
4	deadlift	2/A/1	____ @ ____ KG	O.K / less / more
		3 min active rest*		
1	pull-up	2/A/1	____ @ ____ KG	O.K / less / more
		3 min active rest*		
2	pull-up	2/A/1	____ @ ____ KG	O.K / less / more
		3 min active rest*		
3	pull-up	2/A/1	____ @ ____ KG	O.K / less / more
		3 min active rest*		
4	pull-up	2/A/1	____ @ ____ KG	O.K / less / more
		cool down*		

*3 min very light arobic exercise, like rowing, jogging, cycling, dancing, shadow-boxing, …

Recovery **Day 91**   R-HR___energy: -

guidelines / what and how to do it:
Probably the best thing to do now is the traditional thai-massage.

If a massage is not availabe, do the joint-mobility-routine.

If you have any muscle-pain, then press the painful point with a foamroller or tennis- / lacrosse-ball for 3 minutes (or more) on it and move on it very slowly.

If you like to do some „sports", or if you have to work physically, then try to stay in „light avtivity".

Remember:

#1 Your heartrate has to stay low, your muscles should not work hard and your passive structures must not be stretched.

#2 keep heart rate lower than BPM: 160-(your age)=_____

#3 If you exercise without a HR-monitor, then do not go harder than you can handle while breathing through your nose. It must feel light / easy to maintain the activity.

#4 Take a look at your rest-heart-rate:

>5 BPM more than normal? Take it easy!

>10 BPM more than normal? You need more than one day for recovery!

Congratulations! You have finished the first big cycle...

Now you have some options, how to continue:

Option 1: **You need more strength (#1 goal).**
Start from day 1 and repeat the complete course. It is possible, that your individual adaptation to strength-training needs individual changes at some parameters. You are free to experiment with that. Some powerlifters increase the range of motion (ROM) from week to week.
For example the deadlift:

Week 1: 90% of your max and 6 steps away from full ROM
Week 2: 90% of your max and 5 steps away from full ROM
Week 3: 90% of your max and 4 steps away from full ROM
Week 4: 90% of your max and 3 steps away from full ROM
Week 5: 90% of your max and 2 steps away from full ROM
Week 6: 90% of your max and 1 steps away from full ROM
Week 7: 90% of your max and full ROM
Week 8: Test your new max
Week 9: 90% of your max and 6 steps away from full ROM
...to be continued!

To *maintain your endurance* during this period, you should do the following and not more:
cardio, 30-90 minutes @ <180 (-age) BPM

Option 2: **You need more endurance (#1 goal).**

Week 1: Performance Test

Week 2: cardio, 30-90 minutes @ 160 (-age) BPM

Week 3: cardio, 30-90 minutes @ 180 (-age) BPM

Week 4: intervals, short bursts with long active rests

Week 5: intervals, short bursts with short active rests

Week 6: Intervals, 3-5 rounds (5 min / 60 sec)

Week 7: Intervals, 3-5 rounds (5 min / 60 sec)

Week 8: Performance Test

Week 9: cardio, 30-90 minutes @ 160 (-age) BPM

...to be continued!

To *maintain* your strength during this period, you should do the following and not more:

Exercise-speed: fast (controlled)   Breaks: 3 to 10 minutes

Set	weight	reps
1	multiply your 1RM by 0,5	5
2	multiply your 1RM by 0,6	5
3	multiply your 1RM by 0,7	5
4	multiply your 1RM by 0,83	5

Option 3: **You want to <u>maintain</u> your level of fitness.**

To *maintain your endurance*,
you should do the following:
cardio, 30-90 minutes @ <180 (-age) BPM
Test yourself sometimes...

To *maintain* your strength,
you should do the following:

Exercise-speed: fast (controlled)   Breaks: 3 to 10 minutes

Set	weight	reps
1	multiply your 1RM by 0,5	5
2	multiply your 1RM by 0,6	5
3	multiply your 1RM by 0,7	5
4	multiply your 1RM by 0,83	5

Test yourself sometimes...

Special: Your strength is O.K., but you want to improve your ability to resist against fatigue.
Take 80% of your 1RM.
Do 10 sets of 2 reps with 60 sec rests.
After this take 60% and do 1 set (amrap).
Every week you reduce the rests for 5 seconds.
After 5 weeks your body will need a break.
For the next cycle you reduce the sets and increase the reps. Stay at a total of ~20 reps.

Week 1:	10 sets x 2 reps @ 80% rest=	60 sec
Week 2:	10 sets x 2 reps @ 80% rest=	55 sec
Week 3:	10 sets x 2 reps @ 80% rest=	50 sec
Week 4:	10 sets x 2 reps @ 80% rest=	45 sec
Week 5:	10 sets x 2 reps @ 80% rest=	40 sec
Week 6:	Recovery-week	
Week 7:	7 sets x 3 reps @ 80% rest=	60 sec
Week 8:	7 sets x 3 reps @ 80% rest=	55 sec

...to be continued!

next cycles: 5 sets x 4 reps
4 sets x 5 reps
3 sets x 7 reps
2 sets x 10 reps
1 set x 20 reps

To *maintain your endurance* during this period, you should do the following and not more:
cardio, 30-90 minutes @ <180 (-age) BPM

THE ESSENCE OF PHYSICAL FITNESS TRAINING

Of course there are a million ways to train.

There are also a million ways to waste your time and energy.

Your goal is to improve your overall fitness.

Now you have a good idea how to train for that goal.

Continue exercising and tracking your work.

This is the right way to improve and maintain strength,

without neglecting endurance, flexibility and joint mobility.

    Save your good health,

        save your time,

            train smart!

Printed and published:
BoD - Books on Demand, Norderstedt
ISBN 978-3-7386-5512-4